T0339820

ADVERSARIAL JUSTICE:

America's Court System on Trial

ADVERSARIAL JUSTICE:

America's Court System on Trial

Theodore L. Kubicek

Algora Publishing
New York

ISBN-13: 978-0-87586-527-0 (trade paper)
ISBN-13: 978-0-87586-528-7 (hard cover)
ISBN-13: 978-0-87586-403-7 (ebook)

Library of Congress Cataloging-in-Publication Data —

Kubicek, Theodore L., 1919-
Adversarial justice : America's court system on trial / Theodore L. Kubicek.
    p. cm.
Includes bibliographical references and index.
ISBN-13: 978-0-87586-527-0 (trade paper : alk. paper)
ISBN-13: 978-0-87586-528-7 (hard cover)
ISBN-13: 978-0-87586-403-7 (ebook)
1. Adversary system (Law)—United States. 2. Justice, Administration of—
United States. I. Title.

KF384.K83 2006
347.73—dc22

                            2006022893

Front Cover: Legal Jousting
Image: © Images.com/Corbis
Creator Name: Dick Palulian

Printed in the United States

To my wife, Margaret

ACKNOWLEDGMENTS

I owe many persons a debt of gratitude for helping me, not with the text (for that I take sole responsibility), but for continually helping me out of a jam because of computer and word processing problems, usually my own fault. Three in particular I should recognize: Tracy Rivinius-Rudish of the Word Processing Department of the law firm of Simmons Perrine Albright & Elwood, P.L.C. gave me some instruction on how to do things better. I was frantic when I called upon Peggy Knott, Assistant to the Dean of the Faculty, Coe College. Her reputation as a word processing expert proved highly deserved. She graciously spent many hours remedying my mistakes so that I could conform to the guidelines of Algora Publishing. Then, when my D drive crashed, Jeremy Crawford MCSE, MCP+1, Information Systems Manager of Stamats Communications Inc., came to my rescue. On all those occasions I aged considerably, always fearful that I would lose several years of work on my manuscript.

Someone always has to be last, but in many respects Martin DeMers was first. As editor of Algora Publishing, he patiently guided me throughout the process of publishing my book. I always appreciated his comprehension, although I was not surprised, since Algora Publishing presents itself as an academic-type press for the educated general reader.

Sincere thanks to all of you.

TABLE OF CONTENTS

PREFACE

It was 1983 at the midyear meeting of the American Bar Association. The topic was whether the association should hire a public relations firm to help improve the image of lawyers. Chief Justice Warren Burger had heard enough. Rising to his feet, "he politely questioned the entire exercise, asking whether instead of offering cosmetic solutions to a professional crisis, it might be better to talk about what the lawyers—not the spinmeisters—might do to help improve the situation....[He then] pointed out that the original role of lawyers was healing social conflict, and that we really needed to embrace that role once again."[1] His words, like those of Harvard Law Dean Roscoe Pound back in 1906, were largely ignored.[2]

In order to comprehend this book, you must understand America's adversarial trial system. Consider this explanation: Two lawyers, one the prosecutor or plaintiff's attorney and the other the defense or defendant's attorney, are sitting at their respective places in the courtroom during a trial. Above them hangs a balloon filled with truth. From the balloon hang two strings, one going to each of the attorneys. It is their joint job, presumably, to pull that balloon

---

1. Preface Journal, May 2004, p. 74
2. See Chapter 1.

filled with truth down for all to see; but that is not the way the system works.

Unfortunately, each attorney also holds a stick. Each stick represents obstruction, falsehood, lies, ambiguity, trickery, confusion, deceit, dishonesty, deception, or possibly perjury. Each stick actually is an arsenal of all kinds of chicanery and stratagem. When the truth balloon begins to descend, if the opposing party feels threatened by its descent, then that party uses his or her stick to push the balloon back up. Consequently, the balloon may never reach its desired landing, leaving the judge or jury unable to make a proper decision, a decision that should be based solely upon the truth, not one resulting from the actions of the lawyer who most deftly uses his or her stick.

Faulting America's adversarial system of justice is not something new. Several writers and speakers have done so, none probably as prominent as Roscoe Pound, Dean of Harvard's Law School. Oddly, though, the usual criticisms about America's judicial system are mostly superficial, rather than salutary. Dean Pound himself, though severely critical of the adversarial system, did not touch upon the heart of the problem. Up to now, no one has comprehensively analyzed what needs to be done to make America's judicial system consistently more trustworthy, thus more reputable.

The difficulty in reform is due to America's traditional adversarial system of justice. Convention has made some legal procedures so sacred to the law profession and the judiciary that it is considered a sacrilege to even mention them, let alone change them. Silence thus is the norm.

America's adversarial system inherited or devised many sacred cows and, for the most part, is content with them. Think of all aspects of the judicial system. Think of judges who sit tall, but mostly silent. Think of handcuffed juries who are generally forbidden to question or speak, and thus are even more silent. Think of trial attorneys who are paid to advocate for their clients, regardless of the factual result. Think of the public itself, any number of whom want the opportunity to avoid liability or guilt in any eventual incident, even though they may in fact be in the wrong. Finally, consider the various lawyers' rules of professional conduct and the pronouncements of the courts, both of which require the trial attorney to zealously advocate and both of which preserve that most sacred cow, the attorney-client privilege of communication. All these factors contribute to America's questionable adversarial system of justice.

It is the last mentioned cow that prohibits ultimate truth in the courtroom. With few exceptions, secrets between attorney and client must be kept, maintain both the Rules and the courts. But, obviously, as long as secrets are kept from the opposing side, truth cannot be assured, even though some trial attorneys maintain that the adversarial system makes it possible to bring, actually laboriously wring, out the truth. It seems odd that the American judicial system, while maintaining that it seeks the truth, forces secrets to be kept so that truth is difficult if not impossible to elicit.

Do not blame trial lawyers as a group for this oddity. They are only following the rules laid down by others, principally the bar and the judges. Not to follow these rules, as preposterous as they are, could cause a mistrial or engender malpractice. Thus this book in part is a plea that the rules and court decisions that mandate the attorney-client privilege in a contested matter be revisited and altered. Any such change in the privilege, however, will be difficult to achieve since, as Milwaukee lawyer Delos N. Lutton states, the privilege "has been a hallmark of the legal systems of developed countries for centuries."[3]

It should be especially noted, however, that this privilege should be abrogated *only* when conflict exists. It should be obvious, but apparently is not, that when parties lock horns, all facts must be placed on the table, not hidden behind some pretext of privilege. It should also be obvious that in the absence of conflict, it is no one else's business what occurs between attorney and client. So there is no misunderstanding, let me specify anything involving a crime is considered a conflict. It is simply asinine to believe that criminals

---

3. www.abanet.org/journal/ereport/albrit.html, April 1, 2005, p. 2

should be allowed to hide behind their attorneys, that their attorneys are their sanctuary, the same or even more so than a church, temple, or mosque.

Certainly all individuals, no matter what their wrong, are entitled to be legally represented, but no client's position should be advocated adversely to the truth. If a trial attorney claims not to know the truth, then it is likely that such attorney has either not tried to find the truth or possibly because the rules and court decisions do not allow the door to be opened to the truth.

This book will not be popular with those trial lawyers who relish the trial game in the courtroom and events leading up to it. They are the ones who love the give and take of this system. They believe, or at least they so state, that only through this system can truth be attained. Yet, if pressed, most trial lawyers will be constrained to admit that their ultimate objective in any trial is winning, in fact winning at all costs. In other words, their real objective is not truth, but winning. That is exactly what their clients want, in fact demand, because that is what they pay for. Actually, then, in America's court system, truth and justice are not synonymous.

Often, these same lawyers maintain that once persons have had their day in court then they have received justice, no matter what the outcome and no matter that the outcome may not be consistent with the truth nor even with the evidence.

Realistically, another problem hovers in the background. Many trial lawyers, as would any other group trying to earn a living, will not gracefully accept change. "Change" as used herein refers to reform in procedures leading up to and including court trials. Change often scares people, because any change might affect their pocketbook. Greed should not be a hallmark of a profession, but it generally is. Speaking especially from the standpoint of the legal profession, this stance is unfortunate. Presumably, lawyer Roberta R. Katz, who with the help of Philip Gold wrote *Justice Matters*, would agree. "The work of a justice system should be less mercenary and more noble; keeping order among individuals for the good of the whole."[4]

The faults of our legal system, mostly attributable to the adversarial system, will be disclosed and then corrective changes will be proposed. Law students, often idealists when entering law school, will discover these faults after they get out in the real world, perhaps even after a few months in the classroom. Maybe the way they are taught changes them. Steven Keeva, an ABA Journal assistant managing editor, wrote this.

> Recent research demonstrates how a majority of first-year students who come to school with an inner motivational focus—that is, a desire to help others, make the world a better place and so on— move rather rapidly to an external focus, such as earning a lot of money or impressing others.[5]

Lawyers and law students are endlessly taught ethics, but these teachings are not concerned with truth in the courtroom but rather with irrelevant matters such as civility, evidentiary matters, trial tactics, lawyers' collegiality, client relationships, so-called professionalism (actually a meaningless word under America's adversarial system), and billing practices.

During my forty years practicing law, I avoided the field of battle known as the courtroom as much as possible as I soon became disenchanted with the adversarial system of justice. Since I spent little time in the courtroom, trial lawyers no doubt will question my ability, even my right, to criticize the US judicial system. My response will always be that one does not need to be a trial lawyer, or even a lawyer, to perceive the obvious flaws in our judicial system. Note, for example, the highly acclaimed writer and senior fellow at the Manhattan Institute, Walter K. Olson.[6]

I have long hoped the judicial system would change, a useless wait so far, although a few, mostly judges and law professors, have questioned the system. These writers have been largely ignored by the organized bar. Regardless of that, this book is an extension of what other writers have noted, in that it advocates many substantial

---

4. Katz, p. 124
5. Journal, November 2003, p. 84. See also, Journal, June 2004, p. 74
6. Olson, in general

changes in the system of justice. Without these changes, there can be no real improvement in our judicial system.

In a way, I have been unfortunate (and thus not always happy with what I observe) in that I have always been a reformist at heart. This makes me look at things critically. In that sense, I am like Vincent Bugliosi, noted prosecutor for eight years in the Los Angeles District Attorney's office, who wrote, "The reader should also note that I am, by nature, a critical person. I'd find fault with a beautiful morning sunrise."[7]

Even though our present judicial procedures are of long standing, still it is doubtful that they will last indefinitely because of their inherent defects. Eventually, failure to admit and correct these defects will result in something much worse, possibly for lawyers themselves. It matters not whom or what to blame. What does matter is that our legal system needs reform before other approaches, probably not to everyone's liking and possibly worse, take its place.

In his book Adversarial Legalism, Robert A. Kagan quotes Albert N. Alschuler. "The civil trial is on its deathbed, or close to it, because our trial system has become unworkable. The American trial has been bludgeoned by lengthy delays, high attorneys' fees, discovery wars, satellite hearings, judicial settlement conferences, and the world's most extensive collection of cumbersome proce-dures. Few litigants can afford the cost of either the pretrial journey or the trial itself."[8]

Reform, herein primarily referring to elimination of the adver-sarial system and its cousin, the attorney-client privilege of commu-nication in conflict matters, will be difficult. No group, professional or otherwise, likes to admit that their way of doing things is defective. Some trial lawyers like to think, and want the public to think, that the US system is above reproach. Jackson, Wyoming, lawyer Gerry Spence has stated that "we (the lawyers) repeat the gospel over and over—to our clients, to ourselves, until it has

---

7. Bugliosi, p. 23
8. Kagan, p. 109

become the liturgy of our lives—that the (judicial) system may not be perfect, but it is the best damned system known to man."[9]

The late Judge Harold J. Rothwax, a long-time veteran of the New York State Supreme Court, said something similar in his book, *Guilty: The Collapse of Criminal Justice.* "In spite of what must be an increasing awareness of these defects and deficits, we somehow, against all the evidence, continue to repeat the mantra that ours is the 'best' system in the world. Whether we say this out of arrogance, ignorance, or inertia is unclear."[10]

Carl Horn III, US Magistrate Judge for the Western District of North Carolina, wrote this in his recent book, *Lawyer Life.* "With the current prevalence of lawyer misery, lawyer-bashing, and lawyer jokes, it is crucial that the legal profession rediscover the 'high calling' and rekindle the ideals that are its prouder heritage."[11]

Lawyer, former judge, and television personality Catherine Crier wrote in her book, *The Case Against Lawyers,* that the "the criminal justice system is in need of a serious house cleaning."[12] In discussing the public's negative attitudes toward attorneys and their behavior, Roberta Katz stated that such feelings "indicate[s] that something deeper must be involved."[13] Katz went on to say:

> The sad fact is, the civil justice system, in its present form, is both dysfunctional and obsolete. Dysfunction and obsolescence make possible the other abuses, and permit those who exploit and misuse the system to make large profits from it.[14]

At least one leader of the bar showed a discomfort with the situation as it now exists. J. C. Salvo, 2005-2006 President of the Iowa State Bar Association, was addressing members of the Iowa State Bar when he wrote the following.

> I'm hopeful that as we begin a new year...that you all will find your practices a little better than before and a little more fulfilling. I say

9. Spence, p. 188
10. Rothwax, p. 233
11. Horn, p. 2
12. Crier, p. 213
13. Katz, p. 29
14. Katz, p. 40

hopeful, because I suspect for some it is neither better nor fulfill-ing...Beginning our new year, we ought to explore not only ways to make the practice of law satisfying and rewarding for our clients and our families, but also ways to elevate the public image of the legal pro-fession.

As we consider where we go from here, we need to assess where we are and where we want to be...we need to continue in our efforts to raise the public image of lawyers. I hear too often that will never happen. "People's opinions of lawyers are low, always have been and always will be, regardless of what we do"....Rather than accept the notion that things are this way, why not dream of a public opinion of lawyers that is better than before and say why not? We need to dream that dream....Let's find ways to do good things better and eliminate things that ought to be gone.[15]

Like most observers of the climate of the legal profession, Salvo understood the underlying dissatisfaction of the practicing profession as well as the public's mood concerning it, but he offered no alternatives. This book reveals why this lawyer dissatisfaction and this public perception exist. It not only speaks to the problems caused by the adversarial US judicial system, but it also offers the solutions necessary to right the wrongs caused by these ancient pro-cedures.

---

15. Lawyer, January 2006, p. 5

CHAPTER 1. THE PREMISE

In judging the US judicial system, no one group should be blamed for its deficiencies. Let's just consider each of the following participants and blame them accordingly:

Lawyers are the players in the judicial game of justice. They make the rules, which are designed to give then a fighting chance whether or not their clients are liable or guilty.

Judges, also lawyers, are either trial judges (who run the show) or appellate judges (who concern themselves with prior legal procedures rather than guilt or innocence).

Juries, when used, generally make the final decision. But their hands are so tied that they are incompetent to do it right.

Perhaps the blame lies with the founding fathers who drew up the US Constitution. Unfortunately, they fouled up—or perhaps it is the Supreme Court Justices who interpret the Constitution.

Finally, the general public is at fault because, fearing that someday they themselves might find themselves in court, they are not anxious to change the system. After all, they want a fighting chance to win even though they actually may be liable in a civil matter or guilty in a criminal suit. With our present system, winning, regardless of guilt or liability, is always a distinct possibility and the public knows that.

Historically, lawsuits were not looked upon favorably. The participants, meaning primarily the parties thereto, were not admired. The lawsuit was thought of as an evil, "destructive of reputation."[16] That is not true today. Now people in general are more litigious. One writer calls it a 'law explosion.' He blames it on our "society as a whole...a general expectation of justice, and a general expectation of recompense for injuries and loss."[17]

Not everyone agrees that we are being inundated with lawsuits. In fact, some lawyers are fearful that systems alternate to court trials such as arbitration or mediation are lessening the need for trials. They maintain that trials, rather reported decisions of such trials, are necessary to inform the public as to what the law of the land is.[18]

In a narrow sense that may be true. But it does not take an adversarial court proceeding as we know it in America to determine what the law is. Any reformation of our trial system would accomplish the same result. And abolishing our contentious manner of conducting trials would raise the stature of trial lawyers, judges, and even juries.

Criticism of our trial procedures, or, more broadly, our judicial system, is not something that has happened over night. In 1906, Roscoe Pound, then Dean of the University of Nebraska Law School and later professor and Dean of Harvard University School of Law from 1910 to 1947, and a most eminent scholar, presented his paper entitled *The Causes of Popular Dissatisfaction with the Administration of Justice* at the 29th annual meeting of the American Bar Association. It is amazing that he spoke this one hundred years ago, not yesterday. This, in part, is what he said.

> The sporting theory of justice, the "instinct of giving the game fare play,"...is so rooted in the profession in America that most of us take it for a fundamental legal tenet. But it is probably only a survival of the days when a lawsuit was a fight between two clans in which a change

16. Olson, p. 2
17. Friedman(1), p. 5
18. Cf. Landsman, pp. 105-110

of venue had been taken to the forum. So far from being a fundamental fact of jurisprudence, it is peculiar to Anglo-American law; and it has been strongly curbed in modern English practice. With us, it is not merely in full acceptance, it has been developed and its collateral possibilities have been cultivated to the fullest extent. Hence in America we take it as a matter of course that a judge should be a mere umpire, to pass upon objections and hold counsel to the rules of the game, and that the parties should fight out their own game in their own way without judicial interference. We resent such interference as unfair, even when in the interests of justice. The idea that procedure just of necessity be wholly contentious disfigures our judicial administration at every point. It leads the most conscientious judge to feel that he is merely to decide the contest, as counsel present it, according to the rules of the game, not to search independently for truth and justice. It leads counsel to forget that they are officers of the court and to deal with the rules of law and procedure exactly as the professional football coach with the rules of the sport. It leads to exertion to "get error into the record" rather than to dispose of the controversy finally and upon its merits. It turns witnesses, and especially expert witnesses, into partisans pure and simple. It leads to sensational cross-examination "to affect credit," which have made the witness stand "the slaughter house of reputations." It prevents the trial court from restraining the bullying of witnesses and creates a general dislike, if not fear, of the witness function which impairs the administration of justice. It creates vested rights in errors of procedure, of the benefit whereof parties are not to be deprived. The inquiry is not, What do substantive law and justice require? Instead, the inquiry is, Have the rules of the game been carried out strictly? If any material infraction is discovered...our sporting theory of justice awards new trials, or reverses judgments, or sustains demurrers in the interest of regular play.[19]

These words, which clearly could be spoken with as much authority today, were a strong indictment of our judicial system. Unfortunately, Dean Pound has been largely ignored, although given some lip service. Perhaps it was because in 1906 he had not yet risen to the stature he acquired in later life. Perhaps those listening to him at the time were fearful of losing their private turf. Years have gone by but times have not changed.

Walter Olson believes that the old views that litigation was expensive and unpleasant, something to avoid, have been replaced by the beliefs that "litigation deters wrongful conduct...a way to

19. Pound, pp. 4, 5

redistribute wealth....Given this new view of litigation, rules discouraging lawsuits ceased to make sense....We opened the door to the 'fishing expedition'...We made it much easier to organize class actions...We dropped many of the rules against lawyers stirring up litigation." [20]

THE AMERICAN THEORY OF LAW: THE GOAL IS WINNING

According to one writer, "three features mark the Anglo-American legal system as different from all others. One is the extent to which our law is formed in litigation...it comes...from the judges...[secondly] we pit antagonists against each other, to cast up from their struggle the material of decision. A third...is the trial by jury."[21] The second feature, that of pitting antagonists against each other, is the important one here. The courtroom is an arena for a contest, even a war, between the opposing parties, not a forum for determining the truth.

This is not the way, however, that some lawyers and judges view the trial, which, they believe, can only result in good. And the mere "prospect of a trial...is enough to winnow the chaff."[22] The West Virginia Supreme Court allegedly stated that "we do an injustice not only to the intelligence of jurors, but to the efficacy of the adversarial system, when we express undue concern over the quantum of collusive or meritless lawsuits....Forged in the heat of trial, few but the meritorious survive."[23]

Elliot L. Bien, civil appellate specialist in Novato, CA, and then President of the California Academy of Appellate Lawyers, would not seem to agree entirely with those conclusions when he wrote that "advocacy is supposed to be helpful, to make it easier for judges to understand the facts and legal issues of the case. Yet too much advocacy today is the opposite of helpful. It favors exaggeration over

---

20. Imprimis, March 2004, Volume 33, Number 3, pp. 2,3
21. Rembar, p. 116
22. Olson, p. 258
23. Olson, p. 259

accuracy, attack over debate, and indiscriminate barrage over efficiency and cooperation. A culture of belligerence has taken root in our legal system."[24]

The US Supreme Court uses the United States Constitution as a pretext for arriving at certain conclusions favored by the Justices. This is particularly true of the due process of law provisions in the Fifth and Fourteenth Amendments. These provisions have been interpreted to include conduct "which 'shocks the conscience,' methods which offend a sense of justice, fair play and decency...(lack) of counsel...personal rights and freedom from personal restraint . . . anything that offends the dictates of reason...[and] secrecy of membership"[25]

No doubt, our Supreme Court has yet to exhaust the inclusionary features of the due process clauses. The rather novel idea that these rights exist has mainly occurred in one generation, although one writer describes these rights as having grown gradually.[26] These decisions broadening the interpretation, and hence the powers, of the due process clauses might not have pleased Justice Oliver Wendell Holmes who in 1930 believed that the "Fourteenth Amendment was not intended to give the majority of the court carte blanche to embody its own economic or moral beliefs in its prohibitions."[27]

It is a sad commentary on American criminal law that our courts' first concern is not the guilt or innocence of an individual but rather with whether the procedure used in proving such guilt or innocence followed arbitrary rules contrived by previous courts. Retired Judge Macklin Fleming, a former justice of the California Court of Appeal, devotes a whole chapter in his book, *The Price of Perfect Justice*, to the irrelevance of guilt.[28] "The phrase 'the irrelevance of guilt' is one used by Lord Diplock of the British House of

---

24. Judicature, November-December 2002, p. 132
25. Fleming, p. 94
26. Olson, p. 272
27. Holmes' dissenting opinion in Baldwin v. Missouri, 281 U.S. 586, 595 (1930). And see Fleming, p. 96
28. Fleming, pp. 121-128

Lords in referring to the American rules of criminal law that require suppression of all evidence obtained by unlawful, improper, or irregular means."[29]

By suppressing evidence allegedly obtained in violation of these rules, the courts believe that police and others will be discouraged from violating these laws as the judges have interpreted them.[30] Perhaps the best-known example is the Miranda rule,[31] which, inter alia, requires an initial police warning to a suspect that he or she has a right to remain silent and a right to counsel. Absent the prior warning, any thing the suspect says is suppressed at trial on the basis that such evidence has been illegally obtained, that is, as that term has been defined by the Supreme Court.[32]

At least one writer believes that the public is dissatisfied "with the administration of criminal justice...[since] our courts have substituted formalism for fairness, and, in the process, they are burying the truth."[33] Another writer states that it is unrealistic to assume that courts are "seeking truth and only truth...especially in the American legal system."[34] Perhaps it is this assumption of seeking truth, and failure to obtain it, that causes dissatisfaction with our court system.

A common and popular saying is that "it is more important to safeguard the innocent than to punish the guilty,"[35] a phrase that actually has the ring of a cop-out. Of course we want safeguards, but that does not mean, ergo, that we should not attempt to punish every guilty person.

Under the adversarial system of justice, ethical lawyers, of whom there are many, believe it or not, are under a distinct disadvantage. They operate under the spirit of the American Bar Association's *Model Rules of Professional Conduct*,[36] actually under their own

---

29. Fleming, p. 121
30. Fleming, p. 121
31. Miranda v. Arizona, 384 U.S. 436 (1966)
32. Coolidge v. New Hampshire, 403 U.S. 443 (1971)
33. Rothwax, p. 235
34. Posner, p. 205
35. Leonard Pitts, syndicated columnist, Gazette, November 18, 1998, p. 2A

state's Rules of Conduct, whereas their opponents may not, in fact, probably do not. Although probably intended to be used in a different sense, the following statement in 1996 by Bob Eaton, now retired but then chair and CEO of Chrysler Corp., later DaimierChrysler, applies to this situation. "There's something wrong when being intellectually honest makes you dead meat for people who aren't."[37]

The *Model Rules* "are intended to serve as a national framework for implementation of standards of professional conduct."[38] However, mere violation of the spirit of the Rules is actually not a violation at all and results in no punishment of any kind. A lawyer's violation of a specific Rule may or may not, generally not, result in any disciplinary action. It depends upon whether the alleged violation is reported, to whom reported, its deemed seriousness, the willingness of a particular bar's disciplinary committee to pursue the complaint, whether the violator belongs to a large or small firm, the judgment of the court that ultimately decides, and the reputation of the violator.

Unfortunately, even the spirit of the Rules is suspect. Consider the following in *Readings on Adversarial Justice: The American Approach to Adjudication* by Stephan Landsman, Professor of Law, DePaul University College of Law, which book was produced under the sponsorship of the American Bar Association Section of Litigation.

> Since the rough-and-tumble of adversary procedure exacerbates the natural tendency of advocates to seek to win by any means available, the adversary system employs rules of ethics to control the behavior of counsel. To ensure the integrity of the process certain tactics are forbidden, including those designed to harass or to intimidate an opponent as well as those intended to mislead or to prejudice the trier of fact. In addition to their prohibitory function, the rules of ethics are designed to promote vigorous adversarial contests by requiring that each attorney zealously represent his client's interests at all

---

36. See Model Rules generally
37. *Newsweek*, "My Turn," September 23, 1996, p. 20
38. Rules, p. xii

times. To ensure zeal, attorneys are required to give their undivided loyalty to their clients.[39]

Any two readers probably would disagree as to their understanding of what was said above. Which is more important, the attorney's behavior or the attorney's zeal in representing the client? If trial attorneys were forced to make a choice between proper behavior and zealous representation in order to win, it is fairly clear which they would most likely select.

Judging from what she wrote, it is doubtful that Catherine Crier is a fan of our present judicial system.

> Litigation firms are clearly bent on winning at all costs...Whether personal injury suits, class actions, or high-profile criminal cases, the trial process is now a game rather than a search for truth and justice. Rules are thwarted, abuses are tolerated, juries are manipulated, all in the name of winning rather than seeking the truth or doing justice. Each time this occurs, new case law emerges, becoming precedent for further perversion of long-standing legal principles.[40]

During the O. J. Simpson fiasco, Ellis Cose, columnist and contributing editor since 1993 for *Newsweek* magazine, wrote that "they [the lawyers] routinely play the disinformation card, the conflicting-experts card, the confusing-statistics card, the character-assassination card, the exclusion-of-important-evidence-because-of-an-illegal-search card. All are aimed at swaying jurors with something other than a straightforward presentation of relevant evidence."[41]

In his book, Professor Landsman refers to the US judicial system as the "sporting theory of justice"[42] and "the modern American race to beat the law."[43] Subsequently, he says "the contest by its very nature is not one in which the objective of either side, or of both together, is to expose 'the truth, the whole truth, and nothing but the truth'."[44]

---

39. Landsman, p. 5
40. Crier, pp. 189,190
41. *Newsweek*, "Shuffling the Race Cards," October 9, 1995, p. 34
42. Landsman, p. 52
43. Landsman, p. 52
44. Landsman, p. 56

Defendants, whether in a criminal or a civil case, are under no duty to disclose facts that would be harmful to them. In other words, defendants may deliberately hide information concerning their case from the plaintiff.[45] Surely, this is in contradiction to the *Model Rules*. Rule 3.3: Candor Toward the Tribunal, thereof, speaks to this but the key words in the Rule are "knowingly," "known," "knows," "reasonably believes."[46] It is doubtful that defendants' attorneys, who are required to be zealous advocates and are paid to win, would ever admit to having knowledge or belief of anything that would be harmful to their client. In our present court system, the defense attorney is not hired to be a disinterested party searching for the truth.

Marilyn vos Savant, *Parade Magazine* columnist, posed the following question and answer.

> Say one party to a lawsuit is truly in the right, and the other is wrong, Can we, as citizens, be confident that the right person will prevail in court?...No, but he or she stands a good chance of either winning outright or obtaining a compromise without bloodshed, which is one of the main reasons for the existence of court systems. Unlike battlefields in wartime, where anything goes, our judicial system attempts to impose fairness on fights without making prior judgments. That handicaps the person in the right, but it handicaps the person in the wrong even more. Nevertheless, the courtroom remains a battlefield: One can be totally in the right and still be outmaneuvered.[47]

Ignoring whether under our system a rightful participant stands a good chance of winning, it is disputable whether the US judicial system attempts fairness. "Fairness" in this sense only means that both parties have equal access to the courts and that both are represented by counsel. When those two requirements are met, then almost anything thereafter is acceptable. Both parties, the one in the right as well as the one in the wrong, are thrown in an arena where those who have to decide, either the judge or the jury, especially the latter, are mere observers. What is fair about that?

---

45. Rothwax, p. 180
46. Rules, p. 76
47. *Parade*, January 8, 2006, p. 20

Richard Reeves, Universal Press syndicated columnist, bemoaned America's attitude, primarily in sports, when he wrote "it's not how you play the game; it's whether you win or lose" and then he quoted Vince Lombardi's well-known statement, "Winning isn't everything; it's the only thing."[48] Those statements could equally apply to our trial system.

Even Professor Landsman admits, "it remains true that the system in its present form is pretty sick."[49]

Mark Hansen, senior writer for the *ABA Journal*, recently wrote that "nobody likes to lose, especially trial lawyers, whose overriding desire to win comes not just from their legal training. It runs through virtually everything in our society...." Then, when discussing high-profile lawyers who claim never having lost a case, he said "such claims give the public the false impression that if they spend enough money to hire the best lawyer, they can't lose."[50] That impression may not be as false as he believes.

Judge Rothwax made the following obvious observations. "Since most defendants are in fact guilty of some or all of the charges, the usual defendant on trial is yearning neither for an accurate reconstruction of the facts nor for an error-free trial."[51] And, "If a defendant is guilty, he should be convicted. If he is not guilty, he should be acquitted. An erroneous acquittal should be a source of dismay, not indifference."[52]

The latter statement is the whole *raison d'etre* for this book.

RESULTS OF THIS SYSTEM

One need go back only ten years or so to note that Presidents of the American Bar Association have been aware that the public is dissatisfied with the system of justice.[53] None of these personages,

48. Gazette, October 26, 2004, p. 4A
49. Landsman, p. 203
50. Journal, May 2005, p. 37
51. Rothwax, p. 135
52. Rothwax, p. 181

however, attribute the causes of dissatisfaction to the adversarial system of justice. It is always something else, such as overcrowded courts, not enough judges, ethnic and racial bias, erosion of rights, lack of resources, complex legal issues, burdensome caseloads, and failure of the legal profession to educate the public.

It is as if they merely want to wash an old, beat-up car (the adversarial system) to cure the ills of the American judicial system. The washing would clean the car of minor headaches but it would not rid it of dents (the adversarial system) nor of rust (the attorney-client privilege in conflicts). They seem to be out of touch when they suggest remedies that would fail to redress the major faults of the adversarial system.

While their suggestions no doubt have some minor merit, it appears that the legal profession is unwilling to face the real reason for dissatisfaction, to wit, "There is no respect for the truth, and without truth, there can be no justice."[54] This lack of respect seems odd since a loser at any trial, whether civil or criminal, would have few sympathizers if such loss were simply the result of determining the truth.

Meg Greenfield, now deceased but former columnist for *Newsweek* and former opinion page editor of the *Washington Post*, wrote that "most of our tedious political and programmatic debates about what we should do to secure justice, law and order are pitifully irrelevant."[55] Under the US system of justice, winning the lawsuit has become the central theme. No lawyer deemed their salt would engage in a trial with an attitude of not winning. Their clients would expect them to do everything possible to win, and they would. Again, truth becomes irrelevant.

From time to time, law professionals make efforts to clean up their act, but rarely at top levels has notice been taken of the dire

---

53. See, e.g., Journal, August 1992, p. 8; Journal, July 1993, p. 8: Journal, September 1993, p. 8; Journal, April 1994, p. 6; and Journal, March 1996, p. 6
54. *Parade*, "We're in the Fight for Our Lives," by Bernard Gavzer, quoting Judge Harold Rothwax, July 28, 1996, p. 4
55. *Newsweek*, Meg Greenfield, "Scandal in the Courts," August 21, 1989, p. 68

results caused by the adversarial system. Consider what Judge Rothwax wrote.

> As we try to make it more fair, the system becomes more time-consuming, more complex, more unknowable, and more uncertain. Truth becomes less central. The issue of the defendant's guilt becomes more and more subordinate. 'Did he do it' becomes lost in the melange of other issues—and the other issues come to dominate not only the trial but the appeal.[56]

Another writer seems amazed that our "Anglo-American legal system [is] different from all others." He describes the system as "peculiar" in "the way we conduct these cases: we pit antagonists against each other, to cast up from their struggle the material of decision."[57] Still another writer has described the system as an "experiment," culminating in "a disaster, an unmitigated failure." He feels that this "unleashing of litigation in its full fury has done cruel, grave harm and little lasting good. It has helped sunder some of the most sensitive and profound relationships of human life."[58] Continuing, he bemoans what he describes as "courtroom combat...[producing]...inflated damage claims and speculative legal theories, scorched-earth procedural tactics and calculated appeals to emotion over reason."[59]

Our courts reflect our social class system. The US judicial system is touted as being open to all. That, taken alone, is true. No one is turned away from using our courts because of race, sex or otherwise. When a need arises, one can go to court to seek redress or to defend oneself. Unfortunately, though, mere need or desire is not enough. Generally, one must be able to afford going to court in order to be successful. Lawyers may refute this. They will recite access to legal aid, pro bono efforts of the bar, contingent fee arrangements, court appointments, or even self-representation (known as pro se litigants) as proof otherwise. As Cedar Rapids educator William C.

---

56. Rothwax, p. 207
57. Rembar, p. 116
58. Olson, p. 2
59. Olson, p. 7

Jacobson wrote, while discussing education, "Our society embraces several truths that unfortunately are not true."[60]

Except for the contingent fee situation, of all the others consider the possible quality of the representation. No matter how conscientious lawyers try to be in these other situations, do you really believe that their work product will be as good as when they are paid much more in private engagements? If you still believe in the affirmative, compare the representation of a corporate giant with the representation of some ordinary working stiff. For starters, realize that the giant would have at least two attorneys, more likely a whole firm, working for it. Stiffs are lucky when even one represents them.

Consider the story reported in the Knight-Ridder newspapers, dateline Philadelphia.[61] The story concerned legal proceedings against John du Pont, the alleged murderer of an Olympic wrestler. At least five lawyers, two psychiatrists and a private investigator represented Du Pont. How much help do you believe that the prosecutor had? Compare the legal representation that persons on the dole or even the working stiffs have working for them.

What made the du Pont story interesting and relevant here were the following comments accompanying the story. "In the utopian world of justice, all things are equal. In the real world, you get what you pay for....How can anyone presume to believe the old folklore that we have a good prosecution, a good defense, and the jury will decide?....It doesn't happen. A good defense costs a lot of money."[62]

In one of her syndicated columns, Molly Ivins wrote, "I doubt it will startle any citizen to read that the quality of justice in this country is deeply affected by how much you can afford to pay for it."[63] Trials are expensive. In part, it is because of the nature of the trial. "All work is custom produced."[64] Elimination of the adver-

---

60. Jacobson, p. 142
61. Gazette, March 16, 1996, p. 1
62. Gazette, March 16, 1996, p. 1
63. Gazette, April 23, 2006, p. 13A
64. Neely, p. 164

sarial system of justice, however, may not reduce the legal costs. The primary reason for eliminating adversarial conflict is not to reduce costs, although it might and it is hoped that it would. Rather, it is for arriving at a just and proper solution based solely upon truth. Regardless, the costs may not seem so great if the decision is based on truth and not on other, irrelevant matters.

"Law is a chancy business at best....Cases appear to be clear until skilled lawyers begin to manipulate the panoply of half-hidden principles that lurk in a body of law eight hundred years old."[65] The uncertainty of results cannot be otherwise when the goal of every trial lawyer is to win, no exceptions. Consider the following comments by Roger T. Stetson, Iowa State Bar Association President, 1996-1997. Note that no reference to the adversarial system of justice is made.

> There is a looming crisis in our justice system. Throughout the country, courts are facing vastly increasing demands and diminishing resources. At the same time, there is a growing lack of confidence that our court system can provide justice for our citizens. A poll conducted last year [1995] by the Gallup Organization for the ABA Journal revealed that while 96 percent of the respondents endorsed the idea that all Americans are entitled to equal justice, only 14 percent believe it is very likely that the goal can be achieved. In a recent survey in Iowa, less than half of the survey respondents said they trust the courts and most believed that the courts give preferential treatment.[66]

In an article in the *ABA Journal* entitled *Mootcourtitis*, Professor James W. McElhaney, the Baker and Hostetler Distinguished Scholar in Trial Practice at Case Western Reserve University School of Law in Cleveland and the Joseph C.Hutcheson Distiguished Lecturer in Trial Advocacy at South Texas College of Law in Houston, as well as senior editor and columnist for *Litigation*, the journal of the ABA Section of Litigation, attributed much of our present woes in trials to the way students are taught in the law schools.

> It's the way they teach the advocacy system....They've turned the advocacy system into the adversary system....If they taught students

---

65. Neely, p. 109
66. Lawyer, September 1996, p. 5

to be advocates instead of adversaries, everybody would be better off....[They've been taught not to] concede anything...or you'll give your case away...there is a dangerous message in the law-school system. It implies that whatever the law says is an issue is worth arguing....[As a result,] some lawyers figure that whatever the other side wants must be wrong, so they always argue the opposite—whatever it is.[67]

Professor McElhaney had more to say about this in the *Journal's* January 1998 issue under the headline, *Over-the-Top Arguments*, later reprinted again in the *Journal*.

There are a lot of different reasons why lawyers push arguments that don't make sense...part of the problem comes from the law itself. The common law in particular seems to have a "whole hog or none" approach to deciding disputes...trained in this kind of thinking, it is understandable that some lawyers feel compelled to argue every question as if it had only one side.

Another source of unreasonable arguments is law school, where you were rewarded with good grades for spotting and articulating every possible legal theory—whether or not it was remotely plausible.

The legacy of that training permeates our profession through the thousands of lawyers who routinely make every argument they can think of.

Another cause of arguments that go over the top is the 'adversary system' itself, which somehow makes lawyers think that the more adversarial they are, the better they are doing their job.

Then there is the marketing factor. Just watch the posturing some lawyers go through in an effort to win and keep clients—especially the lawyers who try to create the impression that they are the meanest dogs in town.[68]

Bar leaders and other law professionals seem to be hypnotized by our judicial way of doing things. Repeatedly they recite how good the system is, such as the following.

Even with the evident problems of the justice system and our profession...our system is still the one the nations of the world, individu-

---

67. Journal, June 1990, p. 68
68. Journal, December 2005, p. 28

ally and collectively, look to as the one to emulate. That is because, for all its flaws, it is the fairest and most successful means that humans have yet devised for peacefully resolving disputes.[69]

As noted previously, Judge Rothwax wondered "whether we say this out of arrogance, ignorance, or inertia."[70]

It is rather tiresome to hear this mantra repeated over and over as if it were the gospel, especially when laypersons, who think otherwise, are tending to abandon our system if and when they can.[71]

Two lawyers have more to say about our present judicial system, the first Roberta R. Katz and the second Robert A. Kagan.

> The system's in bad trouble now. Its problems are structural. And it's time for the next restructuring, if the system's fundamental principles are to be preserved and strengthened...and if Americans are to find in their courts, once again, the quality of justice they expect and require.[72]

> Compared to the usual defendant, wealthier, better-educated, better-connected defendants enjoy many advantages...the inequality arises from the capacity of well-financed defendants, or of especially dedicated defense lawyers, to create an entirely different kind of legal proceeding by mobilizing all the weapons afforded by adversarial legalism.[73]

THE NECESSITY OF CORRECTING SYSTEM

Lawyer Katz ably grasps the problems arising from the adversarial American system of justice.

> There is a growing sense that the court system is not working properly, and therefore a growing distrust of law...As citizens, concerned about the integrity of the system, we know that something is wrong. We're worried. We ought to be. In fact, we should be appalled by the growing popular opinion that justice is no longer being served in the courts."[74]

---

69. Journal, April 1994, p. 6
70. Rothwax, p. 234
71. Journal, August 2002, p. 38
72. Katz, p. 7
73. Kagan, p. 93
74. Katz, pp. 15,16

And,

> One of the primary functions of the adversary system is to let the litigants get their information to the decision-makers. But if the decision-makers cannot understand what the litigants and witnesses are saying, then the adversary system has been compromised at best, and at worst rendered useless.[75]

And,

> When any institution no longer upholds the principles it was established to uphold, it's time either to abandon the principles or change the institution. To abandon the principles of neutrality, objectivity and rationality is unthinkable. The institution must be changed.[76]

And,

> Before crisis turns to catastrophe, it will be necessary for the present generation of leaders, in the bar, the courts, the legislatures, and the law schools to get involved. This means that many of them will have to master their own understandable fears: of new technologies; of threats to self-interest; of reluctance to change an inherently conservative institution such as the law; of reticence in the face of inevitable opposition from colleagues; of the very enormity of the task.[77]

The repetitive stance of the bar, or at least of its leaders, "that the system may not be perfect, but it is the best damned system known to man,"[78] makes it difficult to correct the system of trying cases. Whether or not one first believes it, if one hears it enough times, one will eventually tend to believe it. Or maybe after it is said innumerable times, it becomes difficult to reverse course to try to find something better, a substitute that relies on the truth and only the truth. No doubt, defense trial members of the bar would be touchy about changing a system that they have long used to earn a living. Yet, "to be a trial lawyer is to see the ignominy of slow justice in a system in which the *process* itself punishes all who come in contact with it: the winner as well as the loser."[79]

---

75. Katz, pp. 127,128
76. Katz, p. 97
77. Katz, p. 158
78. Spence, p. 188

Professor Landsman admits that "the system is not without its faults...[but feels that] the most frequently advanced criticisms of the adversary system are not well founded."[80] He does not identify what these "advanced criticisms" are. Then he suggests what "most likely" would be the alternative, judge participation.

Judge Rothwax stated "that the American courtroom is dangerously out of order."[81] It might have been better if he had said that "our system of justice is dangerously out of order." It is true, of course, that all illegal, or alleged illegal, activity culminates in the courtroom, but the activity itself may have occurred long before. Thus it really is not only the courtroom that is out of order, although it is there that such prior activity is examined with a microscope for defects.

So what do defense attorneys do? Actually, what are defense attorneys supposed to do, or required to do? Should they determine the truth of the charges, likely resulting in their client's conviction, or, in the alternative, should they hide damning facts, likely resulting in their client being found innocent? Easy answer. "Right and wrong has nothing to do with it [the system] anymore."[82]

A New York City judge would agree. "Criminal justice in America is in a state of collapse....We have formalism and technicalities but little common sense."[83] At first glance, it would appear that 1993-1994 ABA President R. William Ide III, agreed when he said "what is needed today is nothing short of a revolution in our administration of justice."[84] Unfortunately, he did not appear to have our trial procedures in mind when he spoke, as he made no mention of our feeble adversarial system in finding the truth.

Three years later another ABA President, Roberta Cooper Ramo, now a lawyer in Albuquerque, New Mexico, although

---

79. Jenkins, p. 437
80. Landsman, p. 33
81. Rothwax, p. 232
82. *Newsweek*, "No Joking Matter," by Bob Eaton, September 23, 1996, p. 20
83. *Parade*, "We're in the Fight of Our Lives," by Bernard Gavzer, quoting Judge Harold Rothwax, July 28, 1996, p. 4
84. Journal, September 1993, p. 8

admitting that lawyers are officers of the court, stated that "lawyers and the legal system are increasingly under attack in the media and on Main Street USA...[because] adults do not understand or value the legal system [and thus] cannot be adequate jurors,"[85] a rather contemptuous attitude toward laypersons. In addition to suggesting public education, she recommended that lawyers fight back, in other words, react to criticism as well as being proactive. To the contrary, it is possible that this public criticism is due to the adversarial system of justice, which she never mentioned. It is quite logical to believe that abolishment of the adversarial system of justice would benefit society as a whole as well as the legal profession in particular.

THE DIFFICULTIES IN CHANGING THE SYSTEM

As long as attorneys in a suit are deemed adversaries rather than advocates or representatives, it will be impossible to change the system. Actually, even the word "advocate" sounds a bit too strong to describe the attorney's position in a lawsuit. The word "representative," to represent, would actually be a better designation.

Retained attorneys should do their best to ensure that their clients are treated fairly, that is, decently, and that they receive everything that their clients are entitled to—but no more. They would then be said to "represent" their clients, which would then entitle them to be properly labeled as officers of the court. When defense attorneys intentionally effect innocent verdicts for their clients who are in fact guilty, then those attorneys cease to be professionals. Those attorneys are more like the lawbreaker they represent and no longer should they be entitled to be labeled as officers of the court. Judges are properly labeled as officers of the court. Lawyers, who brazenly take advantage of the adversarial system to

---

85. Journal, March 1996, p.6

secure a verdict of innocence, regardless of the evidence, should not be graded at the same level as judges.

As is mentioned more than once, bar leaders constantly complain about perceived problems in our judicial system. Mostly they are quite amiss, skirting the issue of what is really wrong with the adversarial system, by complaining about chronic underfunding,[86] or talking about overcrowded courts and prisons and racism in our justice system.[87]

At least one bar leader, former ABA President Ide, seemed to have an open mind to change. "The [justice] system is in crisis and within this crisis lies the opportunity for a reform that will serve our nation well into the next century. All we need do is grasp that opportunity."[88] Unfortunately, he offered no solutions. Certainly, he did not specifically address the adversarial nature of the US system of justice. That omission is not surprising, for it is common.

In a 1976 speech, Warren Earl Burger, then Chief Justice of the US Supreme Court, said this. "What we seek is the most satisfactory, the speediest, and the least expensive means of meeting the legitimate needs of the people in resolving disputes. We must therefore open our minds to consideration of means and forums that have not been tried before."[89] Although he offered some solutions, he, too, failed to address the adversarial system of justice. Again the typical failure.

Lawyer Katz observed that "legal reform still remains more a hot topic than an effective movement...proposals are interim measures at best."[90] Later, she said the following.

> The proposals address many aspects of the current system: ethical standards, procedural reforms, the roles of judge and jury, the nature and extent of damage awards, and the uses of Alternative Dispute Resolution. But it's important to remember that the adversary system consists not merely of a thousand different human bits and procedural pieces. It's made of three interacting major components: the

86. Journal, ABA President J. Michael McWilliams, July 1993, p. 8
87. Journal, ABA President Talbot "Sandy" D'Alemberte, August 1992, p. 8
88. Journal, May 1994, p. 8
89. Journal, June 1976, p.727
90. Katz, pp. 81,82

parties involved (clients and attorneys), the decision-makers involved (judges and juries), and the rules and procedures involved.[91]

To her credit and unlike many other critical observers, Katz offers her version of solving some of the problems resulting from America's adversarial system of justice. She suggests that the courts of general jurisdiction be more fragmented into what she labels as CORE courts, these new courts to be based upon subject matter, such as the present tax and bankruptcy courts.[92] However, she sidestepped the basic problem, our adversary system of justice. Eliminating the adversary system would eliminate the problems that she and others enumerate from time to time.

Surely, the faults that exist in this judicial system are often caused or created by our US Supreme Court. Their decisions are paramount. Whatever they decide, the "subordinate state and federal courts follow,"[93] which in and of itself is as it should be. If a new issue, or something judged to be a new issue, arises, the US Supreme Court ultimately decides, this assuming that the issue is deemed a Constitutional issue. Rarely in recent years, though, has the Supreme Court not deemed an issue to be a Constitutional one.

Consider how nonsensical the US Supreme Court has become. "It undertook in Anders v. California to analyze the duty of appointed appellate counsel. Because of the requirement of equal protection of the laws contained in the Fourteenth Amendment, said Justice Clark, appointed counsel may no longer advise the court that the appeal has no merit."[94] In his decision rendered in 1967, Justice Clark wrote as follows.

> The constitutional requirement of substantial equality and fair process can only be attained where counsel acts in the role of an active advocate in behalf of his client....Of course, if counsel finds his case to be wholly frivolous, after a conscientious examination of it, he should so advise the court and request permission to withdraw. That request must, however, be accompanied by a brief referring to anything in the record that might arguably support the appeal....This pro-

---

91. Katz, p. 87
92. Katz, p. 125
93. Fleming, p. 95
94. Fleming, p. 74

cedure will assure penniless defendants the same rights and opportunities on appeal—as nearly as is practicable—as are enjoyed by those persons who are in a similar situation but who are able to afford the retention of private counsel....(386 US 738, at pp. 744-45).[95]

Constant complaints are made that our courts are clogged. It cannot be otherwise when the US Supreme Court itself not only condones frivolous lawsuits, it forces lawyers to pursue them in Appellate Court. Under the Anders case, the counsel may "withdraw." That only means that another lawyer must take his or her place. The original lawyer, under those circumstances, must first prepare and file a "brief," presumably so that some subsequent lawyer has reason to take over. Now all of this is regardless of the truth or the facts, no matter what occurred at the trial level. The subsequent lawyer thus must take an adversarial posture and pursue the case even though it is a waste of time for the entire judicial system. As Judge Fleming points out, "in evaluation of these claims innocence or guilt of the defendant becomes largely immaterial."[96]

Although the US system of justice has largely evolved from the English system, English Justices have adopted a more common sense approach than our Supreme Court Justices. "English courts evaluate the problem of suppression of evidence as one of striking a balance between the individual's interest in freedom from intrusion and society's interest in maintaining order and suppressing crime, and purely technical violations of...Rules do not foreclose the use of evidence obtained in violation of the Rules."[97]

The English Rules referred to above are so-called Judges' Rules that instruct the police as to how to act and perform their duties. But even if the police violate these Rules, the English courts still determine whether to suppress the evidence so obtained. Such evidence is not automatically thrown out as in America.

---

95. Fleming, p. 74
96. Fleming, p. 74
97. Fleming, p. 127

CHAPTER 2. JUSTICE

THE THEORY

John Rawls, distinguished Professor in the Harvard Philosophy Department before his death, devoted a whole book to *A Theory of Justice*. In it, he stated that his "guiding aim is to work out a theory of justice."[98] His approach is more philosophical than substantive and thus of little value for purposes here. One of the better dictionaries[99] seems to associate "justice" with "truth." So would many lawyers and judges. Although not synonyms, surely the words "justice" and "truth" are closely related, or at least they should be. If "justice," though, is deemed the goal of every trial, then it is obvious that under the US system "truth" and "justice" are not synonymous. Allegedly, the aim of every trial is to establish the truth of the controversy. However, when truth favors the other side, then the party possibly harmed by the truth will choose to ignore it, sidestep it, or distort it.

---

98. Rawls, p. 3
99. *The American Heritage Dictionary of the English Language*, Third Addition, Houghton Mifflin Company, Boston New York (1992)

In his book, *An Introduction to the Law,* C. Gordon Post posed the question, "What is justice?" and this was his response.

> To describe the symbol of justice (the classical goddess of justice, Astraea) is a simple matter; to define justice is another matter. Like Pilate, who asked "What is truth?" and turned away not waiting for an answer, many a lawyer would ask, "What is justice?" knowing full well that no definitive answer was forthcoming. A judge may say "My business is not justice; it is the law." A lawyer might say to a client, "The justice of your claim is clear—now let us see what the law has to say about it."...Justice, or the lack of it, is inherent in two factors instrumental in the legal resolution of disputes: one is the system itself; the other is the men who administer the system.[100]

Two US Supreme Court Justices, of different eras, had this to say about justice, according to the authors of *Justice vs. Law.*

> "I am always suspicious of an advocate who comes before the Supreme Court saying this is a court of justice; it is a court of law."
>
> — Attributed to Justice Oliver Wendell Holmes

> "The suggestion that the function of the judge is to deliver justice, in the sense of meting out what he personally conceives to be justice, quite apart from the Constitution or law, I would have to reject."
>
> — Justice William H. Rehnquist[101]

These statements by eminent jurists surely must be disappointing to laypersons, most of whom no doubt associate truth with justice or, conversely, attribute justice to truth. Maybe, though, one should consider what the two jurists are referring to. Law is a necessary ingredient of any civilized society. Without law, society would be in chaos. To prevent disorder, rules must be made and kept. Professor Rawls described it this way.

> A legal system is a coercive order of public rules addressed to rational persons for the purpose of regulating their conduct and providing the framework for social cooperation.... The legal order is a system of public rules addressed to rational persons....The rule of law also implies the precept that similar cases be treated similarly.... A legal system must make provisions for conducting orderly trials and hearings; it must contain rules of evidence that guarantee rational

---

100. Post, p.10
101. Hickok, Foreword

procedures of inquiry. While there are variations in these procedures, the rule of law requires some form of due process; that is, a process reasonably designed to ascertain the truth.[102]

Note how "truth," "law," and "justice" are intertwined. One cannot long discuss one without soon mentioning one or both of the others. At least most cannot. Oddly, Dean Pound, in his scholarly paper on the dissatisfaction of administering justice, never once mentioned truth as one of the factors. He was solely concerned with the adversarial system as affecting justice. Apparently truth, or the lack of it, did not figure in his appraisal of the system that he questioned. Pound described justice as being "the end of law," an "ideal compromise between the activities of each and the activities of all in a crowded world."[103]

"Law" is too broad a term to be interchangeable with the terms "justice" and "truth." Whereas, justice has a broader meaning than truth, law refers to many facets of the administration of justice. "In the end, the law is not simply about justice. It is about procedure, about rules and regulations and jurisdiction, about the nature of precedent."[104]

It is doubtful that many think of law in terms of justice or truth. Law is thought of as the "rules of conduct"[105] laid down by a governing body (supplemented, of course, by judicial decisions) to control and determine behavior, although whether one has violated the law is ultimately determined by truth in a court of law. At least that is the theory. Note the following by Professor Rawls.

> Imperfect procedural justice is exemplified by a criminal trial. The desired outcome is that the defendant should be declared guilty if and only if he has committed the offense with which he is charged. The trial procedure is framed to search for and to establish the truth in this regard. But it seems impossible to design the legal rules so that they always lead to the correct result. The theory of trials examines which procedures and rules of evidence, and the like, are best calculated to advance this purpose consistent with the other ends of the

---

102. Rawls, pp. 235-239
103. Pound, p. 2
104. Hickok, p. 78
105. Post, p. 7

law. Different arrangements for hearing cases may reasonably be expected in different circumstances to yield the right results, not always but at least most of the time. A trial, then, is an instance of imperfect procedural justice.... Injustice springs from no human fault but from a fortuitous combination of circumstances which defeats the purpose of the legal rules.[106]

In his book, *The Price of Perfect Justice"* Judge Fleming points out that, especially in criminal cases, the appellate courts have become devoted to the idea—or should it be ideal—of perfectibility in the lower (trial) courts. These higher courts do not concern themselves with the substance of the trial but with the procedures leading up to and including the trial. They nonsensically search for mistakes in the proceedings that do not even relate to the guilt or innocence of the accused. As a result, almost any error in the procedures justifies, in their minds, the overturning of the judgment or conviction entered in the lower court. What they are saying, in effect, is that the procedures must be perfect; otherwise the defendant has not been given a fair shake. Judge Fleming, bemoaning that "the ideal of justice [has been] transformed into an ideal of correct procedure,"[107] states that "the consequences have been disastrous."[108]

Sometimes lawyers tell the truth. Actually, most of them do. But Miami attorney Ellis Rubin once said, hopefully somewhat face-tiously, "our justice system is a contest between lawyers as to which one can tell the biggest lie and manipulate the truth."[109] William Faches, a former Linn County Attorney in Cedar Rapids and now deceased, would probably have disagreed. Writing a guest column in the *Cedar Rapids Gazette*, he said, in part.

> Justice is such an elusive concept. Courts of law do not deal with justice, nor do they claim justice is done when a verdict is reached. Courts of law attempt to get at the truth.... the trial of a case is an adversary proceeding. It is a battle—a war.... The important consider-ation in our criminal justice system is not whether the accused com-mitted the crime, but whether the government or the state has proved

---

106. Rawls, pp. 85, 86
107. Fleming, p. 9
108. Fleming, p. 5
109. Journal, February 1990, p. 29

beyond a reasonable doubt the accused is guilty. Whether the defendant actually committed the crime is irrelevant if the burden of proof
is not carried by the government.... The only requirement of the attorney [for the defendant] is to conduct himself in an ethical manner and
play by the rules. He must not succumb to acting illegally.[110]

Laypersons might be shocked at some of what he said, particularly the part about guilt or innocence being irrelevant. The point of
his article, however, was to show that even the guilty are entitled to
be represented by an attorney who, Faches naively presupposed,
would always be acting honorably.

Agreeing with Clarence Darrow, who once said that "there is
no such thing as justice. In fact, the word cannot be defined," lawyer
Gerry L. Spence added, "Most of us maintain vague notions of
justice, but its precise meaning escapes us until we are deprived of
it."[111]

So-called "justice" has, or should have, its limits. The endless
parade of appeals, for instance of those on death row, irks appellate
judges as well as prosecutors. The issue here is not as to the right or
wrong of death sentences, but rather as to the taking up of time of
the appellate courts in endless appeals. According to Judge Fleming,
former Judge J. Edward Lumbard of the US Court of Appeals,
Second Circuit, reported as follows.

For all our work on thousands of state prisoner cases I have yet to
hear of one where an innocent man had been convicted. The net result
of our fruitless meddling in search of the non-existent needle in the
every-larger haystack has been a serious detriment to the administration of criminal justice by the states.[112]

One might ask, if their meddling is fruitless, then why do they
do it? The problem is that all courts, federal and state alike, are at
the mercy of the US Supreme Court. Once that hallowed court
hands down a decision setting forth new "law," then all inferior
courts, state and federal alike, must follow suit. That, in itself, is as
it should be. Until its latest decision, which is deemed a precedent,

---

110. Gazette, November 27, 1997, p. 6A
111. Spence, p. 5
112. Fleming, p. 27

is overturned by some subsequent like court, it is the "law of the land." So Judge Lumbard, like all other judges, was stuck with doing something that might be quite disagreeable. Lower court judges do not like to be reversed, so they follow the "law." Guilt, under those circumstances, thus becomes irrelevant.

THE SUBORDINATION OF TRUTH

In the American concept of justice, truth has many enemies. "Justice" should demand a level playing field, but the rules greatly favor the accused. The accused is given every opportunity to beat the system. In effect, then, the field is not level. Whereas the prosecutor in a criminal trial must reveal almost everything beforehand, the accused needs not—and will not—reveal anything except what it intends to use at the trial.[113]

The prosecution must perform perfectly, as determined by higher courts, whereas the accused is under no such restraints. If the accused wins at trial level, that is the end as well as the beginning, since "the People can't appeal an acquittal, but the defendant can appeal a conviction."[114] If the accused loses at trial level, he or she has every right to appeal. Upon such appeal, it is the prosecution that is under the gun, not the other way around. Upon appeal by the defendant, if the appellate court finds that a mistake has been made, the accused is entitled to a retrial, regardless whether the defendant was actually harmed by a mistake in the lower court.[115]

So the accused has at least two opportunities to beat the system, the prosecution only one. Actually, the accused has almost continuous opportunities to beat the system, as appeals and retrials can be almost endless.

Professor Landsman says something quite odd. See if you would agree.

---

113. Rothwax, p. 179
114. Rothwax, p. 211
115. Rothwax, p. 216

> "Truth is not the end the courts seek. Truth is nothing more than a means of achieving the end, justice. The disclosure of material facts is not the only means of achieving justice, and to treat it as the end is to open the way to unsavory abuses [not identified]."[116]

C. Steven Yerrid, a noted trial attorney of Tampa, Florida, would not agree, if he believes what he stated in a summation to a jury.

> "Let's forget the lawyers' fancy jargon used over and over in this courtroom. The search here is simply for the truth. The truth is no stranger. You can almost always tell the truth when you hear it. It is so easy to recognize. And when it comes to you, you realize it is something you knew all along."[117]

In another jury summation, Yerrid described the courtroom as "this sacred house of truth."[118]

It is possible, of course, that if not all the material facts are presented, an innocent person is just as likely to be convicted as a guilty person. Professor Landsman's statement is confusing unless he contemplates that only one party—the prosecution—need disclose all the facts. If it is not information that the courts seek, then it must be misinformation. And if neither, then the court busies itself with nothing. No wonder "justice" cannot be defined.

Justice, however defined, clearly would want to know whether the accused committed the alleged crime. The accused himself would know the answer better than anyone else. But the Fifth Amendment to the US Constitution says "nor shall any person...be compelled in any criminal case to be a witness against himself." That is understandable since "compelled" could refer to the use of force and force itself could lead to torture, not something that a civilized nation would or should contemplate. Surely an innocent person would not refuse to give his side of the story. Most people would think so and thus it would seem that the prosecutor could comment on an accused's failure to testify during final arguments. Not true, said the US Supreme Court in 1965.[119] In 1981, the same

---

116. Landsman, p. 27
117. Yerrid, p. 211
118. Yerrid, p. 303

Court took it one step further by holding that, if requested to do so by the defendant, the trial court must instruct the jury that no inference can be drawn from the defendant's refusal or failure to testify.[120]

Those who defend our adversarial system of justice seem to have difficulty in justifying their viewpoint. Consider this statement by Ann G. Sjoerdsma, a lawyer and an editorial columnist and book editor for *The Virginian-Pilot* in Norfolk, Virginia.

> Although Simpson did not 'murder' Nicole Brown or Ron Goldman, he did cause their deaths. The court system does not seek truth; it seeks accountability. 'Kill,' a non-legal term, is not the same as "murder."[121]

Judge Rothwax presumably would have disputed her and those of like mind. He was quoted as saying that "there is no respect for the truth, and without truth, there can be no justice."[122] In his book, *Guilty*, Judge Rothwax made a statement that perhaps explains why. "Even when an accused person is brought to trial, there is no guarantee that the process will lead to truth-seeking. Any defense attorney worth his salt will make the case a test of strength, not truth."[123]

It becomes tiresome to repeatedly hear that justice should be distinguished from truth, that the system is not designed to establish the truth, only to grant justice. Apparently, if truth emerges at a trial it is only through mere chance, since it is not sought, at least by an accused, unless it is to the accused's advantage.

Good trial attorneys, especially those defending criminal defendants, will artfully try everything in favor of their clients, other than trying to find out what really happened. They use every device to confound the outcome, since it is their legal duty, as the system now exists, to prevent the accused from being found guilty. Con-

---

119. Griffin v. California, 380 U. S. 609 (1965)
120. Carter v. Kentucky, 450 U.S. 288 (1981)
121. Gazette, February 16, 1997, p. 7A
122. *Parade*, July 28, 1996, p. 4
123. Rothwax, p. 26

trarily, it is the prosecutor's duty to try only for conviction, something, though, that few prosecutors would undertake unless first convinced of defendant's guilt.[124]

Truth, of course, in and of itself does not solely justify a conviction. Maybe the accused was deemed insane at the time of the crime. Maybe there were truly mitigating factors, such as self-defense. Maybe the alleged crime was accidental. But all of these possibilities are determined by truth, not justice. These possibilities have to do with the fairness of the system, something desirable whether or not an adversarial system exists.

According to Judge Rothwax, "about 90 percent of the people who go to trial in this country are guilty."[125] Defense attorneys, of course, know this. But the adversarial system of justice requires these attorneys to "push the envelope."[126] Consequently, the prosecution has the burden to overcome all the obstacles placed in its path by the defense attorney. This game hinders the search for truth, which at best becomes secondary.

Judge Posner believes that one of the difficulties for discovering the truth is because only those cases where truth is difficult to determine are taken to court, in other words, tried before a judge or jury.[127] In view of the fact that defense attorneys have many ways of avoiding the truth and thus often will go to court regardless of the evident facts, Judge Posner's postulate seems somewhat suspect. Even if guilt is quite self evident, what has a defendant to lose by going to court? The defendant can receive no greater punishment by doing so. It is much more likely that an accused goes to trial because of an inability to make a deal with the prosecutor.

Judge Rothwax believed that it was the US Constitution that "was exquisitely designed to impede or prevent the truth from ever seeing the light of day."[128] Possibly, though, it is not the Constitution, but rather the interpretations given to it by the US Supreme

---

124. Rothwax, p. 131
125. Rothwax, p. 130
126. Rothwax, p. 130
127. Posner, pp. 209, 210
128. Rothwax, p. 132

Court. No doubts should exist that the Constitution was framed to protect the rights of the innocent, but it should be equally doubtful that the framers intended that the guilty be given more rights than they deserve. By that is meant that guilty persons should never be permitted to escape lawful punishment, regardless of good or bad procedures leading up to their arrest and conviction. Such procedures, however, should never include inhumane or torturous treatment.

US District Judge Thomas Lambros of Ohio instigated a process known as the summary jury trial in 1980. In this process, "a jury from the court's pool renders an advisory, nonbinding verdict,"[129] after the parties' attorneys make their presentations. It is revelatory that "lawyers who have criticized the process say they don't feel comfortable laying their cards on the table during what could, if settlement goals fail, amount to a dry run before a real trial with real consequences."[130] It is doubtful that such critical attorneys are really interested in finding, actually revealing, the truth.

Three last thoughts, According to lawyer Crier, "there is little attempt to discover any truth but only to win the argument."[131] According to Judge Rothwax, "what is the possibility of justice without truth? Does it not become a pointless exercise if truth is so subordinated that the likelihood of its emerging is remote?"[132] And, according to lawyer Katz, "if this country has come to define justice as that which results from 'clever maneuvering,' we surely have come a long and dangerous way from our ethical and political roots."[133]

---

129. Journal, October 2004, p. 18
130. Journal, October 2004, p. 18
131. Crier, p. 219
132. Rothwax, p. 31
133. Katz, p. 45

THE RESULTS

An editorial that appeared in *The Cedar Rapids Gazette* after the Oklahoma City bombing pointed out how important it was that the accused receives a fair trial.[134] Although not defined, hopefully by "fair trial" it was meant that the suspect be represented by counsel, no matter how odorous that might be to the suspect's attorney. Any other meaning given to "fair trial" would be highly suspect.

Eminent trial lawyer F. Lee Bailey had this to say about fair trials.

> Our deification of the notion of a 'fair trial' has so far submerged the value of an accurate trial that the latter has no real legal significance. That a trial be 'fair' ought to be a minimum standard, not an ultimate objective: someone ought to have the temerity to ask whether the result was correct, not simply whether the rituals were acceptable.[135]

Increasingly, according to lawyer Paul Shectman, former New York State Director of Criminal Justice, the New York Court of Appeals has taken "the view that a criminal defendant is entitled not only to a fair trial, but to a perfect one."[136] This is not an aberration strictly confined to New York courts. "We have built an elaborate set of barriers that the prosecution must surmount before it can arrive at a conviction that will stand up on appeal. It is an obstacle course, a struggle from start to finish."[137] As in any game, it is possible that prosecutors will make a mistake here and there. Chances are that one or more of those mistakes create reversible error. And back goes the case to be tried again, if the prosecutor is so inclined.

The adversarial trial system opens wide the doors to all kinds of irrelevant but successful trial tactics on the part of defense counsel. This is what Nashville trial attorney Alfred H. Knight had to say about this when describing the tactics of the O. J. Simpson defense counsel.

---

134. Gazette, May 4, 1995, p. 4A
135. *Newsweek*, January 2, 1978, p. 7
136. Rothwax, p. 216
137. Rothwax, p. 228

These tactics were far from novel or creative. They are as old as the adversarial trial system and are as frequently used as the financial resources of defendants will permit. They are based on a simple and long-understood syllogism: The job of defense counsel is to create doubt; delay, complexity, and confusion create doubt; therefore, it is the job of defense counsel to create delay, complexity, and confusion.[138]

This is not as likely to happen if the adversarial system were changed to an inquisitorial procedure.

The adversarial system seems to have created another nightmare. While state courts, at least at the trial level, are concerned with the substance of the allegations, federal courts, if appealed to on the same matter, are concerned only with the technicalities and the niceties of the state trial. In these instances, whether or not the defendant is guilty does not concern the federal courts. Listen to what Judge Fleming had to say about this.

Federal jurisdiction over a controversy is now created by the mere allegation of unconstitutional restraint.... In recent years a number of justices of the Supreme Court have adopted the view that because federal law is superior to state law, lower federal courts are superior interpreters of federal law to even the highest state courts. From this premise, the conclusion is drawn that lower federal courts may overrule the highest state courts whenever a question of federal law is involved.... These developments have brought about the current phenomenon of two systems of courts operating simultaneously on the same subject matter, and the ensuing tug of war, waste, confusion, and plain muddle are painfully evident.... Lower federal courts...suffer the weakness of being one-interest courts—courts which concern themselves exclusively with protection of personal rights and privileges and not at all with performance of personal duties and obligations.[139]

Problems exist with state appellate courts as well as with federal courts, the similarity between the two being quite evident. In neither instance are these two judicial systems concerned with the substance of the case, the guilt or innocence of the defendant. These two appellate courts busy themselves with procedures and

---

138. Knight, p. 261
139. Fleming, p. 151

whether or not such procedures pass muster—at least from their viewpoint. Here are what some observers say about this.

> Laymen are invited to believe that our legal system enshrouds the trial process with an escalating system of checks and safeguards called appellate courts, which will correct affronts to justice. This is unmitigated nonsense, as all seasoned trial lawyers and jurists know, and many unwary litigants have learned painfully. Appellate courts have only one function, and that is to correct legal mistakes of a *serious* (in their view) nature made by a judge at a lower level.[140]

> In appellate review of cases involving the dichotomy of right to counsel and right to self-representation, the guilt or innocence of the defendant becomes wholly immaterial. To paraphrase Cardozo, if the trial judge blunders, the accused goes free.[141]

> The basic problem of review or appeal is how to avoid doing everything over again—which would be a tremendous waste—but at the same time make sure that lower-court mistakes are corrected...These "errors" rarely went to the heart of the matter. The appeal system suffered from what Roscoe Pound has called "record worship"—an excessive regard for the formal record at the expense of the case, a strict scrutiny of that record for "errors of law" at the expense of scrutiny of the case to insure the consonance of the result to the demands of the substantive law.[142]

The US Supreme Court seems to be in love with the postconviction review. According to this court, "conventional notions of finality of litigation have no place where life or liberty is at stake and infringement of constitutional rights is alleged."[143] Note the key words "constitutional rights is alleged." That is all it takes, those magical words. If nothing else, this creates delay and of course there is always the chance that the Supreme Court will agree, not too unlikely in this day and age. As Judge Fleming points out, the courts' review or reviews change the "thrust of the litigation...from an accusation against the defendant to an accusation against the court, the district attorney, or some public official."[144]

---

140. F. Lee Bailey, *Newsweek*, January 2, 1978, p. 7
141. Fleming, p. 77, referring to Cardozo in People v. Defore, 150 N.E. 585,587,588 (N.Y. 1926)
142. Friedman(2), p. 149
143. Sanders v. United States, 373 U.S. 1,8 (1963)
144. Fleming, p. 52

With further reference to the multiplicity of suits following trial, Judge Fleming made these observations.

> The consequence of this mechanical proliferation and duplication of the elements of the judicial process has been a corrosion of the sanctions within our legal system and a weakening of the law's power of compulsion.... [145] [And] "The characterization of a criminal proceeding as retroactively unconstitutional and void seriously reflects on the integrity and honesty of the law and suggest to those previously convicted that the law is a fraud and they are its innocent victims.[146]

An editorial in *The Cedar Rapids Gazette* stated that "the thought of the guilty going free remains repulsive in the court of public opinion."[147] A public opinion poll during the O. J. Simpson fiasco indicated the public's discouragement with our judicial system.[148] During the same period, an *ABA Journal* article stated that the trial "has shown them [the public] some of the extremes of vigorous prosecution and zealous defense.... Austin Sarat, a lawyer and professor of law and social thought at Amherst College in Amherst, Massachusetts is quoted as saying this: 'What I think these numbers suggest is the public at large wants to focus on, Did he do it or didn't he do it?' Any deviation from that focus—to violation of rights or 'technicality'—bothers people.'"[149] Obviously, the public unwittingly is referring to the adversarial system of justice. They don't like it when they see it in its raw form. And they shouldn't. It cannot help but reduce their respect for lawyers, judges, juries, and the whole court system.

According to Judge Rothwax, "The aspect of our criminal justice system that frustrates people the most is that it seems so rife with game playing."[150] Although speaking in another context, Judge Rothwax described law as a lottery.[151] The thought of the US

---

145. Fleming, p. 89
146. Fleming, p. 15
147. Gazette, April 1, 1997, p. 4A
148. Lawyer, November 1994, p. 8
149. Journal, October 1994, pp. 53-55
150. Rothwax, p. 121
151. Rothwax, p. 104

judicial system as either a game or a lottery is repulsive, that is, repulsive to everyone except those trial lawyers who revel in the system. Winning, like in any game, is important to them regardless of the consequences. In this context, compare adversarial to inquisitorial and consider which would bring the most respect to the legal profession.

CHAPTER 3. ADVERSARIAL SYSTEM

ADVERSARIAL JUSTICE EXPLAINED

As mentioned earlier, the brazen remarks of our bar leaders that this judicial system is the best in the world have never been proven. It is extremely doubtful that any of these eminent leaders really know whether that statement has any semblance to truth. Our world consists of over 200 nations, each with their own judicial system or manner of settling disputes and punishing wrongdoers. No comparative study of all these systems has been found. It is doubtful that any advantage would be gained by making such a study, unless it would be for trying to support the arrogant claim that the US system is the best in the world.

America's adversarial system of justice has always been with us. Professor Landsman, no doubt believing it to be true, adopted the premise "that the adversary system and the right to a jury trial are recognized as fundamental parts of the American trial system."[152] Another writer described this system as "ugly...to watch," but said it is "the very basis of liberty."[153] That statement

---

152. Landsman, p. 120
153. Journal, June 1995, p. 76

presumptively assumes that any other system denies liberty, a doubtful statement at best. Author-lawyer Richard Neely, former Chief Justice of West Virginia, believes that "all countries are prisoners of their history. America is a prisoner of its love of adversary relationships."[154]

What is meant by "the adversary system," which this book chooses to call "adversarial justice"? Former Professor Lon Fuller of Harvard Law School once described it as follows.

> The expression 'the adversary system" can be used in a narrow sense. When we speak of 'the adversary system' in its narrow sense we are referring to a certain philosophy of adjudication, a conception of the way the trial of cases in courts of law should be conducted, a view of the roles that should be played by advocates and by judge and jury in the decision of a controversy. The philosophy of adjudication that is expressed in 'the adversary system' is, speaking generally, a philosophy that insists on keeping distinct the function of the advocate, on the one hand, from that of the judge, or of the judge from that of jury, on the other.[155]

That, indeed, is in a narrow sense. That definition could describe any system that employs a jury in decision-making. The O. J. Simpson trial comes closer to illuminating what the adversarial system is all about. Professor Landsman has his own explanation of the adversarial system.

> The central precept of the adversary process is that out of the sharp clash of proofs presented by adversaries in a highly structured forensic setting is most likely to come the information upon which a neutral and passive decision maker can base the resolution of a litigated dispute acceptable to both the parties and society.... The key elements in the system [are] utilization of a neutral and passive fact finder, reliance on party presentation of evidence, and use of a highly structured forensic procedure.[156]

Lawyer Katz chooses to describe the court system in this manner:

> The American civil justice system is primarily an adversarial system, pitting a plaintiff against a defendant and letting them and their

---

154. Neely, p. 252
155. Landsman, p. 47
156. Landsman, p. 2

counsels present their best evidence and arguments in accordance with required procedures and standards. In theory, and generally in practice, the system is passive, although this has been changing a bit in recent years. Unlike an inquisitorial system, which actively seeks out cases and evidence, the civil adversary system waits for someone to bring a complaint, then requires the other party to respond. In most cases, by the time a trial opens, an enormous amount of work has already been done. The courtroom provides the climactic confrontation and leads to the decision-making functions of the jury and the judge.

The present adversary system assigns different yet equally important substantive roles to the judge and the jury. In general, the jury is required to decide the facts of the case. The judge determines which laws are relevant to the case. But "facts" and "law" are not always obvious.[157]

Stephen Saltzburg, Professor, George Washington University School of Law, adds that "an adversary system assumes that competing litigants are capable of protecting their respective interests by presenting their cases to the trier of fact in an effective way."[158] More revealing of the adversarial system are the following comments by Charles Maechling Jr., retired Professor of Law at the University of Virginia.

The simultaneous harshness and ineffectiveness of the American system stems in part from a major and little-explored root—the adversarial nature of our courts. All European countries except Great Britain and Ireland, and nearly all Third World countries with a European cultural heritage, employ variation of the so-called inquisitorial method, which is rooted in the 2,000-year tradition of the civil or Roman law. Only the Anglo-Saxon countries cling to a judicial parody of the medieval tournament—lawyers for the state and the defense fight for the body of the accused before a judge as umpire and a jury carefully selected for its ignorance of the personalities and issues before it.... As every first-year law student learns, the function of the trial is not to establish the truth: It is to provide the prosecution with a forum to convince the jury beyond a reasonable doubt that the accused is guilty of the specific crime he is charged with, and nothing else.[159]

---

157. Katz, p. 23
158. Landsman, p. 117
159. Journal, January 1991, pp. 59,60

Still more revealing of our adversarial system are the following comments by lawyer Marvin E. Frankel, a former Federal District Court Judge of the Southern District of New York, and an out-spoken critic of the system.

> We enthrone combat as a paramount good. The "adversary sys-tem," as we call it, is not merely borne as a supposedly necessary evil. It is cherished as an ideal of constitutional proportions, not only because it embodies the fundamental right to be heard, but because it is thought (often) to be the best assurance of truth and sound results.... We are taught to presume as a vital premise the belief that 'partisan advocacy on both sides,' according to rules often counte-nancing partial truths and concealment, will best assure the discovery of truth in the end. We are not so much as slightly rocked in this assumption by the fact that other seekers after truth have not emu-lated us.[160]

Professor Landsman admits that "the adversary process has not, as a whole, been made the immutable law of the land by incor-poration in the Constitution.... The text of the Constitution does not specify what form of judicial procedure shall be used in the courts of the United States."[161] He then states that Article III of the Constitution and the Fifth, Sixth, Seventh, and Fourteenth Amend-ments thereto "require," "seem to call for," and "suggests" an adver-sarial proceeding. He concludes by stating that "constitutional endorsement of the adversary system makes change particularly inappropriate.[162]

Interestingly, lawyer Katz also uses the term "immutable," when discussing our adversary system.

> While the adversary system enshrines and reifies certain basic principles which must be kept, none of the system's components, in their present form, is immutable. In fact, serious change is necessary in order to preserve the principles and virtues of the system. So it has been throughout legal history. So it is today.[163]

---

160. Landsman, p. 54
161. Landsman, p. 36
162. Landsman, pp. 36,37
163. Katz, p. 18

Actually, Constitutional support for the adversarial system has come about only by way of interpretation. The US Supreme Court has stated that "the [Sixth] Amendment constitutionalizes the right in an adversary criminal trial to make a defense as we know it."[164] Ethics Professor Monroe H. Freedman of the Hofstra University School of Law, also chooses to interpret the Constitution in that manner.

> The Constitution has committed us to an adversary system for the administration of criminal justice. The essentially humanitarian reason for such a system is that it preserves the dignity of the individual, even though that may occasionally require significant frustration of the search for truth and the will of the state. An essential element of that system is the right to counsel, a right that would be meaningless if the defendant were not able to communicate freely and fully with the attorney.[165]

These arguments for the adversary system would fall flat, if we enjoyed the inquisitorial system of justice rather than the accusatorial system of justice, which some of our leaders and our appellate courts are so in love with. The US Supreme Court has stated, for instance, that "the preservation of an adversary system of criminal justice [is] the fundamental purpose of the Fifth Amendment."[166] Note that this is only the Court's arbitrary interpretation of the Amendment, it having no basis in fact.

Lawyer David M. Elderkin of Cedar Rapids once wrote that "the fault (of the judicial system) does not lie with the system. It lies with an abuse of the system."[167] Does not it seem odd, though, that a system that is so easily and constantly abused is so well thought of, at least in some circles? Lawyer Elderkin continued. "Ours, with its roots in the English common law, has been the envy of the world."[168] This is similar to puffing that ours is the best in the world. If so, why haven't other countries emulated us, especially those countries that

164. Faretta v. California, 422 U.S. 806, 818 (1975)
165. Landsman, p. 207
166. Garner v. United States, 424 U.S. 648, 655 (1976)
167. Gazette, July 17, 1994, p. 7A
168. Gazette, July 17, 1994, p. 7A

have recently sprung into existence? Even England, where our system first developed, has backed off the adversarial system.[169]

Elliot Bien perhaps comes closest to what Elderkin was trying to point out. In an article in *Viewpoint*, published by *Judicature*, Bien expresses the belief that bar codes or sanctions will not solve the lack of professionalism. This is what he sees is happening because of their failure.

> Codes and sanctions have had a fair trial as remedies for the decline of professionalism. It is high time we acknowledged that those remedies have failed. We must deploy more sophisticated and powerful remedies or our cherished adversarial system will continue its decline into a shouting and shoving match. The public and its elected representatives, already hostile to our system of justice, will not tolerate such a circus for very long."[170]

Bien continues by suggesting that it should be the courts that lay down the rules, presumably because lawyers would be powerless to resist such judicial action. But unless the courts abrogate the adversarial system and its sister, the attorney-client privilege of communication (*only* in court cases), then the courts' actions would be futile.

Professor Landsman quotes Professor Stephen Saltzburg as saying.

> The American adversary system not only recognizes the desire of litigants to win, but it actually relies on the desire to motivate litigants to produce evidence and to develop legal theories for consideration by the decision-maker.... They may want to win even though they know that they should lose.... [This] circumstance is most likely to produce improper behavior, since a person who wants to win when he should not may need to cheat to have a chance to win. If the adversary system works well, its rules should make winning difficult for the person who should lose.[171]

A client pays his attorney to win. As a result, that lawyer will not "throw the game" by helping the opposing side who may not, for instance, have found the deciding law point in an obscure court

---

169. See, generally, Journal, January 1991, pp. 59, etc.
170. Judicature, November-December 2002, p. 132
171. Landsman, pp. 69, 71

opinion. Monetary motivation to win makes it easier to lie, furnish half-truths, confuse with side issues and detractions, and cloud the record with irrelevant evidence. Under this system, a trial lawyer has no desire to make a completely honest presentation, especially if any of it could be detrimental to the client. And even if lawyers want to be honest, their clients won't allow them to be honest if the suit could be lost as a result.

As is well known, "many doctors mistrust the American adversarial system of justice... [In this system, they] believe they're just getting the best presentation instead of getting to the truth."[172] However, the medical profession is approaching the adversarial system in the wrong way, in that they want to limit damages resulting from their alleged mis- or malfeasance. Assuming the medical profession is in fact getting a raw deal because of the adversarial system, they should want to abolish the adversarial system and tout the inquisitorial system.

Some hope may be in the distance. Cedar Rapids and Iowa City defense attorney Charles Nadler thinks that we might be changing from the British adversarial system to the French inquisitorial system. "We seem to be shifting over to the French system, where you do not have the right to remain silent."[173]

A few trial lawyers themselves are giving evidence of hope. Circuit Judge William Schma of Kalamazoo County, Michigan, talks about this in an *ABA Journal* article.

> Some [lawyers] come in and ask to talk to me, and sometimes they end up in tears.... They've matured enough to no longer enjoy the fight. They've got no lust for it anymore. They've gotten themselves in a box and come to feel that what they do day to day is crap." According to the article, Judge Schma believes that "these lawyers simply get caught in the intensity of the adversary system, which gnaws at them.[174]

---

172. Journal, March 2005, p. 40
173. Gazette, June 22, 2004, p. 6A
174. Journal, April 2005, p. 80

APPLICATION OF ADVERSARIAL SYSTEM

> Criminal law has to do with relations between the misbehaving individual and his government, civil law with relations among individuals.... The criminal law establishes rules of conduct; their breach, if prosecuted and if conviction follows, results in punishment.... In a criminal case, the government is a litigating party, "the prosecution".... The civil law seeks to enforce the claims of individuals (or entities) upon each other.... The outcome of a civil case...is usually not punishment, it is a remedy...The criminal law...is not directed to redress of the victim's loss.... The criminal law establishes prohibitions thought necessary or beneficial and through penalties tries to enforce them.[175]

While most comments throughout this book seem to apply to our criminal system, keep in mind that the adversarial system applies equally to our civil procedure. Whether it is a criminal or civil case, all parties—plaintiffs, prosecutors, and defendants alike—desire to win. "Any assertion that the goal of the adversarial process in a criminal case is different from its goal in civil litigation must be rejected. The goal of criminal trials is to impose liability on those whom the substantive law indicates have committed crimes. The goal of civil cases is to permit liability to be imposed according to substantive principles. To say that the criminal case is unique is to confuse the goals of the process with some of its elements."[176]

One does not go into court to determine which party should win. Rather, one goes into court, or is dragged into court, with the goal of winning, on the one hand to either prosecute successfully or to avoid prosecution, and on the other hand to either prove liability or to avoid liability. No matter who the party is, that party desperately wants to win, unfortunately at all costs.

Writer Walter K. Olson had this to say about the usual fracas in the courtroom.

> The law school commentators in their abstract way describe the modern trend in legal procedure, evidence, and jurisprudence as being to encourage the "free and full exploration of a dispute." More bluntly, it is to let the lawyers beat up on each other and each other's clients to

---

175. Rembar, pp. 37,38
176. Professor Saltzburg in Landsman, p. 71

the utmost degree, in hopes that the hotter the fray the more truth and justice will emerge.[177]

Think about that last part about truth. Surely, both parties are not seeking the truth since one of them is sure to lose if the truth does come out. It is possible, although probably not frequently, that initially neither party knows what the truth is, but once truth emerges, if it ever does, the losing party seldom, if ever, throws in the towel. No matter how many times the losing party is knocked to the floor, he or she will get up again and continue to fight, always hoping for some miracle. Don't necessarily blame the lawyers, however. Not many clients are likely to surrender before the fight is over. As one *ABA Journal* article says, "The adversary attitude some-times is encouraged or even demanded by the client."[178]

Another *ABA Journal* article refers to the accusatorial process as a mock tournament, which, it alleges, is prejudicial to the accused. "Since the prosecution needs to build a bulletproof case beyond rea-sonable doubt, it tends to accumulate only information that rein-forces the initial presumption of a suspect's guilt, and to disregard or discount information that contradicts or qualifies it."[179]

Professor McElhaney, in his usual semi-serious fashion, points out that the adversarial system is designed to "have each side present its own evidence and attack the other side's case" so that the judge and jury are "in the best position to make a rational decision between the two.... [the lawyers are pushed] to the polar extremes.... They deliberately overstate their positions"[180]

Overstating a position is only part of the story. Perjury is deemed to be "an unavoidable byproduct of an adversarial litigation system."[181] Professor Freedman once stated that "while lawyers should never condone or encourage perjury, they should argue aggressively the position of their clients, even if they suspect the tes-timony used is perjured. 'We must recognize that the adversarial

---

177. Olson, p. 245
178. Journal, June 1989, p. 74
179. Journal, January 1991, p. 60
180. Journal, March 1996, p. 86
181. Journal, May 1995, p. 72

system was designed to cope with misrepresentation.... Credibility of a witness is a question for the jury.'"[182] That naïve statement assumes that juries are smarter than the rest of us. Although juries are a necessary ingredient of a free society, they sometimes render unfathomable decisions. Consider the Stella Awards, for instance. Stella Liebeck is the one who successfully sued McDonald's when she allegedly spilled hot coffee on herself. Juries are "awarded," when their decisions cannot intellectually be explained.

According to Wendy Kaminer, a lawyer, social writer, and contributing editor of *The Atlantic*, in order for the adversarial system to work you need "good people in every role: a good defense attorney, a prosecutor with integrity, a good judge, a good appellate court...[all who are] thinking, feeling moral people and everyone does his or her job."[183] In other words, every officer of the court must be morally good and perfect in order for the adversarial system to work. That, a mere hope, is expecting too much.

John Langbein, Professor of Law, Yale University, addresses this when discussing equality of representation. "The simple truth is that very little in our adversary system is designed to match combatants of comparable prowess, even though adversarial prowess is a main factor affecting the outcome of litigation."[184]

Judge Frankel would concur. "The person who is 'right' should win. But that is very far from assured in the kind of contest we have been considering. Where skill and trickery are so much involved, it must inevitably happen that the respective qualities of the professional champions will make a decisive difference."[185]

Professor Deborah L. Rhode, Stanford Law School, is also critical of the theory that the adversarial process is best for determining truth.

---

182. Monroe H. Freedman, Howard Lichtenstein Distinguished Professor of Legal Ethics at Hofstra University School of Law, Hempstead, N.Y., in Journal, May 1995, p. 72
183. Kaminer, p. 164
184. Landsman, p. 63
185. Landsman, p. 58

The most obvious difficulty with this premise is that it is neither self-evident nor supported by any empirical evidence...we have [then quoting Geoffrey Hazard, Reporter for the Model Rules Commission] "no proof that the adversary system of trial yields truth more often than other systems of trial." [Continuing] Neither is it intuitively obvious that truth is more often revealed by self-interested, rather than disinterested, exploration.... Why assume...that the fairest results will emerge from two advocates arguing as unfairly as possible on opposite sides? That is neither the way most countries adjudicate controversies, nor the way other professions conduct factual inquiry. Nor is it how the bar itself seeks truth in any setting outside the courtroom. In preparing for trial, for example, lawyers do not typically hire competitive investigators.[186]

The adversarial process supposedly is designed so that the truth can be determined by listening to both sides of the story and then a third party, the listener or observer, a judge or a jury in other words, makes a decision. Unfortunately, that is not the way it actually works. Trial lawyers are not passive advocates. As a matter of pride and for the benefit of the client, the trial lawyer passionately attempts to win, all the while ignoring facts adverse to the client. Zealous advocacy is used as "a justification for making arguments that either confuse material issues or trigger jurors' prejudices on subjects such as race, sexual orientation, ethnicity and religion. Sideshows are cropping up everywhere"[187]

One lawyer, defending the adversarial process, stated that "dirty tricks were not only necessary to litigation, but a badge of expertise."[188] Indeed, "some lawyers rationalize behavior that compromises decorum as a natural, if perhaps unfortunate, byproduct of the adversarial system of litigation"[189] With the adversarial system, "each side present its own evidence and attack the other side's case—making the strongest arguments they can. It's supposed to put the judge and jury in the best position to make a rational decision between the two...[this] helps push the lawyers to the polar extremes of the case"[190] One extreme is to load the trial with

---

186. Landsman, p. 188
187. Journal, October 1995, p. 57
188. Journal, January 1993, p. 112
189. Journal, June 1995, p. 101

questionable evidence. "For the right fee, [expert' witnesses] put their sometimes dubious credentials behind farfetched theories of liability, giving a sympathetic jury some scientific base to support a hefty award," the practice of which is referred to as "junk science."[191]

This system of justice has apparently produced a callous group of defense attorneys. One public defender stated that "after two years [as a public defender], my conscience no longer requires such justification [e.g., to help the defendant into drug rehabilitation]. It doesn't matter to me whether my client really committed a crime. My job is to advocate, and that means I must present the evidence in the way most beneficial to my client.... My goal is to expose reasonable doubt."[192]

The stranglehold that the adversarial system has on our form of trials can be a huge detriment to society. Consider, for instance, a dispute between husband and wife. Lawyer Rudolph J. Gerber, former Judge of the Arizona Court of Appeals, describes use of the adversarial system "for a couple to untie their knot...[as not] as humane as using mediation and arbitration."[193] Yet, where a bitter dispute between a marital couple is involved, an alternate form of settlement is rarely used. In fact, it may be impossible due to the statutory requirements for a dissolution of marriage (divorce). Ethically, two lawyers must be involved. In such an instance, the first lawyer contacted is prohibited from representing both sides—by talking to both parties and suggesting counseling, for example. Under the US system the first lawyer, if acting alone, is not to be trusted. It takes two lawyers, both of whom presumably are then trustworthy, and thus a bad situation is likely to get worse.

In addition, consider the cost to society of indigent defendants charged with a crime. Rather than go through the drudgery of an adversarial trial, usually a plea agreement is reached. If the defendant is in fact guilty, then society may be harmed. If the

---

190. Journal, March 1996, p. 86
191. Journal, October 1991, p. 104, which reviews the book, *Galileo's Revenge: Junk Science in the Courtroom* by Peter W. Huber
192. *Newsweek*, July 13, 1998, p. 14
193. Journal, January 1993, p. 112

defendant is in fact not guilty as charged, then harm to the defendant is clear. Neither result should be desired by society. A system should be designed that clearly benefits all of society all the time, not just some of society some of the time.

JUSTICE VS. TRUTH—THE FAIR TRIAL SYNDROME

One wonders whether trial lawyers would exalt the adversarial system if it were not for the law schools. Law school "training is generally adversarial, and based on rigid rules. Some people are born adversaries, some get that way in law school. Most of the emphasis in law school is on total victory. It teaches how to use the rules to win the game, the battle of wits. It programs lawyers to think in terms of rights and duties and money judgments. Forget common sense."[194]

During the Simpson trial, lawyer David Elderkin wrote that "whether O. J. Simpson is guilty or not, he is entitled to a fair trial before an impartial jury. If this is impossible, and it may well be, it is not the fault of the system. It is the abuse."[195] Clearly, the system was abused. One wonders what Elderkin meant by a "fair" trial. Would he consider the trial to have been fair since the system was abused? However, something deeper than that should be considered. If the adversarial system can be abused so easily, and it probably is every day somewhere, is that a system that should be coveted and maintained?

Former Professor Maechling had this to say about our trial system. "As every first-year law student learns, the function of the trial is not to establish the truth. It is to provide the prosecution with a forum to convince the jury beyond a reasonable doubt that the accused is guilty of the specific crime he is charged with and nothing else."[196] This statement is a bit misleading. No decent pros-

---

194. Journal, June 1989, p. 74
195. Gazette, July 17, 1994, p.7a
196. Journal, January 1991, pp. 59,60

ecutor proceeds to trial or even to indictment until he or she is rea-sonably convinced of the truth of the charges. Once that is determined the prosecutor proceeds to make a case. The truth is embodied in the presentment.

Wendy Kaminer speaks from the point of view of the defense attorney. "Lawyers are taught to have tunnel vision, to focus on par-ticulars—the interests of their clients—instead of the general public good. Not that they don't care about justice, in general (some do, of course), but they will argue that it's best served when lawyers advocate for their clients without passing judgment on the merits of their cases or characters. Both defense attorneys and prosecutors are, therefore, often in the position of defending the indefensible."[197]

Cedar Rapids lawyer Carroll J. Reasoner, former president of the Iowa State Bar Association, lamented that "although a search for the truth is the very basis of our legal justice system...[it is difficult] to judge the facts.... Our legal system asks judges and juries to view evidence which is always conflicting and to decide what is the truth."[198] Her statement is probably more accurate when applied to civil cases than to criminal cases. It is true that in any court trial the evidence presented is conflicting, made so, however, by the actions of the trial attorneys, not ordinarily by the facts if they were pre-sented fairly and accurately. Defense attorneys, mostly in criminal cases, are not anxious to determine the facts, that is, the truth. They will always maintain that it is up to the court, either the jury or the judge, to determine the truth, but, of course, they will do everything possible to obfuscate the truth.

Professor William T. Braithwaite, then associate professor at Loyola University School of Law but now a Tutor at St. Johns College, Annapolis, Maryland, does not seem to agree with many trial attorneys when he wrote that "a political science teacher at a major university recently said to me, 'It is distressing to talk with lawyers and judges who can't tell the difference between the truth and winning an argument.' Thus we should remind students that

197. Kaminer, p. 163
198. Lawyer, June 1992, p. 4

while the able advocate can argue either side of a case, there are, nevertheless, enduring standards of right and wrong by which to judge the things clients and lawyers say and do."[199]

Lawyers in rural communities are more likely to agree with that statement. Annette J. Scieszinksi, then a lawyer in a small Iowa town but now an Iowa District Court Judge, wrote that "clients, who often take their cues for conduct from their lawyers, need to understand that, in litigation, the goal of the adversarial process is fair representation in a quest for justice; and the path to justice is discovery of the truth."[200] It is doubtful that so-called big city lawyers would agree. For instance, lawyer Elderkin, who practices law in a much larger Iowa city, wrote this.

> Our system of settling controversies is adversarial, the trial of a lawsuit is a form of combat. The idea that the adversary system does not arrive at justice is not very thoughtful. In the broad sense, it is not supposed to. It is supposed to resolve disputes. Justice is in the procedure, providing a forum which gives the algebraic maximum satisfaction to the contesting parties. As far as the end result is concerned, justice is subjective. It is one thing to a client and one thing to that client's adversary, it may be something different to a jury by a six-to-two vote, something different to the trial judge and something different to an appellate court, sometimes by a five-to-four vote.[201]

Judge Rothwax, a most vigorous opponent of America's present system of determining justice, had this to say. "If a trial is not a search for truth, what is its point?...The way the adversarial system presently works not only *diminishes* the possibility of truth, it *encourages*, and fosters excess on the part of the lawyers vying for the upper hand. The goal has become victory, not truth."[202]

Judge Frankel, another critic of this system, agrees.

> The claim that our adversary process is best for truth seeking has qualifications and limits recognized by its staunchest proponents...we have again the high authority of Supreme Court pronouncements noting that lawyers in the process are often expected,

---

199. Journal, September 1990, p. 73
200. Journal, June 1995, p. 119
201. Lawyer, November 1995, pp. 20,21
202. Rothwax, pp. 132,133

with all propriety, to help block or conceal rather than pursue the truth. These endeavors are commonly justified in the service of interests that outweigh truth finding—interests in privacy, personal dignity, security, autonomy, and other cherished values...the American version of the adversary process places too low a value on truth telling...we have allowed ourselves too often to sacrifice truth to other values that are inferior, or even illusory.[203]

Judge Posner tries to find a reason why truth is not the one and only goal of our judicial system. "I do not mean that the American system is uninterested in factual truth, but only that the goal of truth is in competition with other goals, such as economy, preserving certain confidences, fostering certain activities, protecting constitutional norms."[204]

Not surprising perhaps, our Supreme Court quotes with approval from a Law Review article. "Under our adversary system the role of counsel is not to make sure the truth is ascertained but to advance his client's cause by any ethical means. Within the limits of professional propriety, causing delay and sowing confusion not only are his right but may be his duty."[205] I wonder whether Justice Rehnquist, who wrote that opinion in 1985, would, upon further reflection, be proud of what he wrote. In no way can one be ethical if truth is not the goal. And surely "professional propriety" does not permit a lawyer to be a cheat.

Professor Freedman, a fan of the adversarial system, has convinced himself that "truth is a basic value, and the adversary system is one of the most efficient and fair methods designed for determining it...the judge or jury is given the strongest possible view of each side, and is put in the best possible position to make an accurate and fair judgment."[206] That is not possible when at least one of the attorneys does everything possible to corrupt the evidence and confuse the court and the jury. Professor Freedman continued. "A trial is, *in part* [author's emphasis], a search for truth...a

---

203. Landsman, p. 55
204. Posner, p. 206
205. Walters v. National Association of Radiation Survivors, 473 U.S. 305, (1985)
206. Landsman, p. 185

trial is far more than a search for truth, and the constitutional rights that are provided by our system of justice may well outweigh the truth-seeking value."[207] It is doubtful that any layperson going to court seeking the truth would agree with that.

The US system depends upon the judge or the jury to determine the truth from what they observe and hear. But truth cannot be determined by a court that barely has a part in the evidentiary process, especially where one or both attorneys make little attempt to present the whole truth.

A writer has stated that it is not the trial lawyer's responsibility to find the truth,[208] although that seems peculiar since a lawyer should try to determine the truth in order to properly prepare for trial, whether or not that lawyer intends to use what he or she finds. If the writer's statement is true, then a party's lawyer is free to present anything regardless of its relevance to truth. No wonder that judges and juries are frequently incompetent to make a finding based upon truth, when the truth is so obscure and actually not deemed very important.

Not so long ago, Tom Schaefer of Knight Ridder Newspapers wrote that "every time you or I justify a lie, we debase what is the God-ordained order for life. As truth is soiled, trust is diminished."[209] Schaefer was not referring to our system of justice at the time he wrote that, but that statement would equally apply to the system. With the adversarial system's unconcern for the truth, not only is trust in our judicial process diminished, but the reputation of the legal profession is surely soiled too.

PUBLIC DISCONTENT WITH SYSTEM

According to Professor Landsman, "Since at least the turn of the century [1900] there has been a lively debate about the value of

---

207. Landsman, p. 184
208. Journal, February 1995, p. 100
209. Gazette, February 4, 2006, p. 10B

the adversary process."[210] According to an *ABA Journal* writer written in 1995 subsequent to the O. J. Simpson trial, "millions of Americans believe they are now personally familiar with the strengths and weaknesses of the adversary process."[211] The writer added that he believed this newfound knowledge could result in a change of our justice system. No change, however, has been noticed. This same Journal writer makes some suggestions that will be mentioned in subsequent chapters but he seems to have missed the real problem when he concludes by saying, "the adversarial system, ugly as it often is to watch, is not a sausage factory, but the very basis of liberty."[212]

Our basis of liberty is not the system of justice but rather its participants: the judge, the lawyers, and the jury, the first two of whom are labeled as officers of the court. Unfortunately, however, under the adversarial system, lawyers do not perform, perhaps even are restrained from performing, as officers of the court. Dean Roscoe Pound addressed this situation as long ago as 1906,[213] but obviously to no avail.

Lawyer Elderkin, although lamenting it, admitted that "there is, I am afraid, a growing effort being made to destroy or curtail the adversary system of settling disputes."[214] As mentioned before, a year earlier he had written, "while it [the Simpson trial] is indeed a sad and tawdry spectacle, the fault does not lie with the system. It lies with an abuse of the system."[215] No one would deny that Simpson's lawyers abused the system, but that abuse, under less scrutiny and no doubt to a lesser extent, occurs somewhere every day. If this system can be so easily abused, it ought to be, and should be, discarded.

Among many, one abuse is that which is called hardball tactics. When litigators think of a trial as a war, then they use any

---

210. Landsman, p. 40
211. Journal, June 1995, p. 73
212. Journal, June 1995, p.76
213. Journal, July 1997, p.94
214. Lawyer, November 1995, p. 21
215. Gazette, July 17, 1994, p. 7A

weapon, legal and maybe not so legal, to fight the battle. Hardball has been defined as "taking the most difficult position for your opponent that your client will live with—and then doing what you say you will do. You never, ever back down."[216]

One writer had this to say about hardball tactics.

> [A] myth is that the closest thing to pure justice is achieved by a contest of hardball litigators. Why on earth, one wonders, should this be so? Scholars are not convinced that adversarial litigation yields a more pure form of justice than other dispute resolution methods. And no one has ever constructed a rationale for believing that the adversarial process is somehow purified by a shouting match.[217]

Unlike the bar, or at least what seems to be a considerable number of the bar, "few lay persons enthusiastically accept the defense lawyer's vigorous advocacy on behalf of those accused of crime."[218]

Dean Pound had more to say about our adversarial system.

> The effect of our exaggerated contentious procedure is not only to irritate parties, witnesses and jurors in particular cases, but to give the whole community a false notion of the purpose and end of law. Hence comes, in large measure, the modern American race to beat the law. If the law is a mere game, neither the players who take part in it or the public who witness it can be expected to yield to its spirit when their interests are served by evading it.[219]

According to Professor Landsman, "criticism of the adversary system is widespread."[220] Geoffrey C. Hazard, Professor of Law, University of Pennsylvania, would agree. "It remains true that the [adversarial] system in its present form is pretty sick."[221]

When one considers that Dean Pound in 1906 addressed the sickness of the system one hundred years ago but the system still exists, it is almost incomprehensible that the system will ever be

---

216. Journal, March 1, 1988, p. 79
217. Journal, March 1, 1988, p. 80
218. Abel, p. 5
219. Pound, p. 5. Also quoted in Landsman, p. 52
220. Landsman, p. 1
221. Landsman, p. 203

changed. Yet some bar leaders are starting to speak up. Jerome J. Shestack, ABA president 1997-1998, stated that "we delude ourselves if we fail to recognize that much criticism of our profession has merit and requires attention."[222]

---

222. Journal, August 1998, p. 71

CHAPTER 4. THE LEGAL PROFESSION

CODES OF ETHICS AND THE ABA RULES

On August 27, 1908, the American Bar Association produced the first set of rules for lawyers. Unless adopted in some form by various state bar associations, these rules, originally called Canons of Professional Ethics or variously as a Code of Ethics, are not mandates for behavior but rather as "professional standards that serve as models of the regulatory law governing the legal profession."[223] They are not "binding on the states, though they serve as a template or basis for most of them."[224] They "are intended to serve as a national framework for implementation of standards of professional conduct."[225] The ABA adopted the present *Model Rules of Professional Conduct* on February 5, 2002. All fifty states and the District of Columbia have adopted rules. "While the Model Rules have no binding effect, they are the basis for most of the state codes that govern professional conduct by lawyers."[226] The "vast majority of

---

223. Rules, p. vii
224. Journal, April 2004, p. 67 and Journal, March 2005, p. 34
225. Rules, pp. xii,xiii
226. Journal, April 2003, p. 32

jurisdictions—44 at last count—base their codes on the *ABA Model Rules.*"[227]

"There are more than one million lawyers in America,"[228] but by no means are all of them members of the ABA. "At no point did more than half the lawyers even bother to join their national association."[229] Practicing lawyers, however, whether or not members of the ABA or of their own state bar, must abide by the Canons or Rules of their own state. Otherwise, they are subject to discipline. This book is only concerned with those who litigate and "only a minority of lawyers spend their time litigating."[230] Unfortunately, though, the general public tends to think of all lawyers as litigators. Thus, when a litigator's malfeasance or misfeasance comes to the public's attention, all lawyers, litigators or not, are tainted with the same distrusting brush.

Professor Braithwaite questioned "do the Rules take their bearings by what most lawyers should do or by what they in fact do?"[231] Relative to client preparation, writer Olson reported that Houston lawyer David Berg wrote that "most of us trim the sail of the testifying client a bit too much...who among us has not warned the client, 'Before you tell me your side of the story, let me tell you what the law is in this area,' or 'If you say that, you'll lose.' Or who, wincing at his client's explanation, has not reminded the client, 'Well, that's not how your boss remembers it,' or 'Aren't you really telling me...?'"[232]

When reading that, surely most litigators squirm a bit, even though the Rules provide an abundance of loopholes. For instance, Rule 3.3, entitled *Candor toward the Tribunal*, provides, in part, "A lawyer shall not *knowingly* [author's emphasis]"[233] do this or that. How easy it is to say, "I didn't know that." Who can refute that?

---

227. Journal, December 2002, p. 46
228. Journal, October 2002, p. 6
229. Friedman (2), p. 690
230. Olson, p. 240
231. Journal, September 1990, p. 71
232. Olson, p. 240
233. Rules, p. 76

Later, the same Rule says, "A lawyer *may* [again, author's emphasis] refuse to offer evidence...that the lawyer reasonably believes is false."[234] The Rules sometimes say "shall" (mandatory) and sometimes say "may" (optional). Note the distinction and how any Rule can be applied accordingly. Presumably, this particular portion of the Rule states "may" because of the conflict between the various Rules.

Relative to perjury considerations, lawyer Joanne Pelton Pitulla, Assistant Ethics Counsel, ABA, had this to say in the *ABA Journal*. "The difficulties arise in determining the lawyer's responsibilities in connection with perjury by a client or another witness. The reason is that professional conduct rules must reconcile two compelling imperatives: first, the prohibition against knowingly offering false evidence to a court; and second, the need for confidentiality between lawyer and client."[235]

Note what the Preamble and Scope of the ABA *Model Rules* states.

> A lawyer's responsibilities as a representative of clients, an officer of the legal system and a public citizen are usually harmonious. Thus, when an opposing party is well represented, a lawyer can be a zealous advocate on behalf of a client and at the same time assume that justice is being done. So also, a lawyer can be sure that preserving client confidences ordinarily serves the public interest because people are more likely to seek legal advice, and thereby heed their legal obligations, when they know their communications will be private.[236]

The term "whistling in the dark" surely must have originated with that quote. Under this system, those listed items can never be "harmonious." It is impossible for a zealous advocate, who is one-sided in outlook and performance, to wear the hat of an officer of the court. The two are totally incompatible and the term "public citizen" is meaningless. Note, too, the qualification "well represented." Would a winning litigant ever admit that the opposing, losing party was not well represented? By making the questionable

---

234. Rules, p. 76
235. Journal, May 1995, pp. 70,71
236. Rules, p. 2

assumption that the opposing lawyer is highly competent, a lawyer can be, in fact will be, zealous and perform in any manner that it takes to win. The Rules back up such a lawyer, because "justice" can then be assumed as being accomplished and the winning lawyer is conscious-free of any wrongdoing.

But consider what *ABA Journal* editor Keeva wrote about this. "Some of the attitudes and behaviors that pass for normal in the legal culture these days are less than conducive to living a balanced, satisfying professional life...ask yourself: What kind of lawyer am I?"[237]

Judge Horn states that lawyers as officers of the court "should embrace ethics, principles, and values far exceeding the *de minimus* requirements of the various Codes of Professional Responsibility."[238] But how can they, if their opponents do not do likewise. Perhaps this is why many lawyers are not happy in their profession.

In this regard, Judge Horn stated that "we have seen that a certain percentage of our brothers and sisters at the bar are miserable. Many others are functioning in [a] 'state of mild torpor...able to continue practicing but certainly not passionate or even enthusiastic about it. Some polls and surveys indicate that a majority of lawyers would not recommend that their own children follow in their professional footsteps."[239]

The existence of the Rules, per se, is not a cause for alarm by those lawyers who wish to violate them. By its own admission, the Rules "simply provide a framework for the ethical practice of law.... Violation of a Rule should not itself give rise to a cause of action against a lawyer nor should it create any presumption in such a case that a legal duty has been breached. In addition, violation of a Rule does not necessarily warrant any other nondisciplinary remedy, such as disqualification of a lawyer in pending litigation. The Rules are designed to provide guidance to lawyers and to provide a structure for regulating conduct through disciplinary agencies."[240]

---

237. Journal, November 2003, p. 84
238. Horn, p. 153
239. Horn, pp. 153,154
240. Rules, pp. 4,5

From this, it can be inferred that the Rules simply provide guidance or a form for states to develop their own Canons or Rules.

Professor Saltzburg, perhaps showing concern for the adversarial system or possibly its participants, wrote that "whether or not changes are made, as long as the process remains adversarial, nothing will be more important than assuring that lawyers perform competently according to the [substantive and procedural] rules governing permissible behavior."[241]

Marvin E. Aspen, Chief US District Court Judge, Northern District of Illinois, wrote that "any notion that the duty to represent a client trumps obligations of professionalism is, of course, indefensible as a matter of law."[242] He then cited a federal case that said the following. "All attorneys, as 'officers of the court,' owe duties of complete candor and primary loyalty to the court before which they practice. An attorney's duty to a client can never outweigh his or her responsibility to see that the system of justice functions smoothly. This concept is as old as common law jurisprudence itself."[243]

Not all trial lawyers and judges feel the same way. Some do, however. San Antonio lawyer William S. Sessions, a former federal judge and former FBI Director, wrote that "duty and obligation to the client and duty to fellow lawyers, as high as obligations may be, fall below that loyalty and deference owed to the court and an unswerving obligation to obedience of the law."[244] At the same time, in quoting Ambassador Sol M. Linowitz, Judge Sessions reminded us that "it was from his role as an officer of the court that the lawyer derived his authority."[245]

At least one court has held that lawyers have a higher duty than what seems to be the ethics prescribed by the bar codes of ethics. According to an *ABA Journal* eReport, "The California Supreme Court, pausing at the intersection of zealous represen-

---

241. Landsman, p. 76
242. Journal, July 1997, p. 95
243. Journal, July 1997, p. 95, citing Malautea v. Suzuki Motor Co., 987 F.2d 1536, (1993)
244. Journal, August 1998, p .62
245. Journal, August 1998, p. 62

tation and malicious prosecution, declared in a unanimous opinion that a lawyer who discovers during litigation that a lawsuit is not meritorious has to drop it or face possible consequences."[246]

The same eReport states that the winning lawyer to the suit said that "the case sends a message that lawyers as officers of the court 'are part of what I think of as a filtration system' to make sure that litigated cases have merit."[247] And, again in the same eReport, "Professor Monroe H. Freedman, an ethics expert at Hofstra Law School in Hempstead, N.Y., says he would be more comfortable with a standard for punishing frivolous litigation that refers 'to a complaint that is false on its face or that is known by the lawyer to be based on false allegations.'"[248] He worries about this since many cases have been won, apparently when they should not even have gone to trial.

Lawyer Shestack makes a point that seems to have escaped the over-zealous trial lawyer when he wrote that "ethical standards should not be treated as articles of containment but embraced as welcome moral principles guiding a growing, vibrant profession. They should lead a lawyer to adhere to standards of practice that are more high-minded and exacting than the rules require."[249] The high profile lawsuits do not indicate that those trial lawyers understand this obligation to their profession.

Some trial lawyers, of course, see it differently. They are not concerned about the public perception of the profession, nor even how non-trial lawyers view their actions. The adversarial process gives them every excuse for being non-professional. Consider this statement from New York City lawyer Ronald L. Kuby. "Defense attorneys have one obligation—to defend the client.... If they tell their client that there is a potential defense that may help the client but say they won't do it, those lawyers are committing malpractice."[250]

---

246. ABA Journal eReport, 5-1-04, p. 1, citing Zamos v. Stroud, No. S118032
247. ABA Journal eReport, 5-1-04, p. 2
248. ABA Journal eReport, 5-1-04, p .3
249. Journal, August 1998, p. 72
250. Journal, October 1995, p. 60

Justifying the adversarial process and the evil that accompanies it apparently is not difficult for advocates of the system. Under the caption *Zealous Representation of Each Litigant,* this is what Professor Landsman says about the system.

> Attorneys have, from the earliest times, been viewed as obstructers of truth. The basis for this view is not hard to identify. Attorneys are skilled advocates. Their facility with words and procedure give them the means of manipulating the information-gathering process. When the advocate lends his talents to the single-minded pursuit of the goals of his client, it is not hard to understand why onlookers might consider him the enemy of veracity. The ethical rule that compels the attorney zealously to represent his client officially reinforces loyalty at the expense of commitment to the search for truth.
>
> In response it should first be noted that attorney zeal is directly linked to party control of proceedings and that the arguments in favor of party control also support zealous representation of the litigant. This is so because the complexity of legal proceedings makes it virtually impossible for parties to proceed without counsel. It has frequently been suggested that the attorney can serve his client and, at the same time, ensure that the truth is disclosed. This position fails to preserve attorney zeal and loyalty because it requires the attorney to act as an agent of the court whenever there is a potential conflict between the client's interest and the pursuit of material information. The likely results of casting the attorney in this impossible situation are unethical conduct if the lawyer chooses to act on behalf of his client in a doubtful case or substantial discouragement of client candor, cooperation, and trust if the lawyer chooses to act on behalf of the court.
>
> This does not mean that an attorney can never be required to act in ways that oppose his client's wishes.... The situations in which the attorney must reject his client's wishes should be clearly and narrowly defined, however, otherwise a chill will be cast over the relationship and over the entire adversary process.[251]

It is unfortunate that Professor Landsman used the term "agent of the court." As an officer of the court, isn't that exactly what a trial attorney should be, an agent of the court? Possibly, in an effort to make his point, he shied away from the proper term, "officer of the court." Failure of trial attorneys to always perform as officers

---

251. Landsman, p. 29

of the court is the whole crux of the two viewpoints. As is obvious, the adversarial process prohibits, or at least inhibits, lawyers from performing as officers of the court. They so act only when it is convenient to do so and not detrimental to their client. But how can a court, whether or not a judge or a jury, reach a fair conclusion if one or both trial attorneys are doing their best to work against truth, in other words befuddle the court and the jury?

Lawyer Michael Higgins wrote in the *ABA Journal* that "ethics rules require lawyers to provide representation that is zealous and competent, not shoddy."[252] The problem is that lawyers, being lawyers or maybe merely being human, would not agree as to what is shoddy. Los Angeles litigator Charles B. Rosenberg wrote that "most people do not understand the adversary system. Or at least they do not understand that, within certain ethical boundaries, lawyers are permitted or even required to advance arguments for their clients even though the arguments may be less than fully persuasive."[253] Surely, this is really being shoddy, which one dictionary defines as "dishonest and reprehensible."[254]

Marilyn vos Savant blames the ill behavior of lawyers not on their conduct, but on what she calls the "principles of the legal profession," in other words its Canons or Rules of Ethics.[255] Perhaps, if blame is to be cast, it should be directed towards some ethics professors, one of whom, Professor Freedman, once stated that "lawyers as advocates have an ethical obligation to raise even distasteful defenses."[256]

A comment in the *ABA Model Rules* states that "lawyers usually defer to the client regarding such questions as the expense to be incurred and concern for third persons who might be adversely affected."[257] This comment continues by saying that if the lawyer

252. Journal, September 1998, p. 22
253. Journal, June 1995, p. 74
254. *The American Heritage Dictionary of the English Language,* Third Edition, Boston-New York, Houghton Mifflin Company, 1992
255. *Parade,* July 23, 1995, p. 14
256. Journal, October 1995, p. 58
257. Rules, p. 13

disagrees with the client then that lawyer may "withdraw from representation." This attorney cop-out frequently appears in the Rules. It presumably preserves the reputation of that particular lawyer, but that procedure does not keep the client honest or preserve the reputation of the profession as a whole. This should matter to the legal profession.

Lawyer Elderkin correctly stated that the rules of ethics "do not require the lawyer to judge the 'morality' of the client's cause."[258] Judge Frankel wrote that lawyers "decide what will be told and what will not be told."[259] An article in *Newsweek* stated that "legal ethics give lawyers considerable leeway to fudge the truth."[260] Albert Alschuler, Professor, University of Chicago Law School, who frequently has been in disagreement with Judge Frankel, wrote that it is "the lawyer's basic function...to serve his client's interest, not retard them"[261]

These comments would seem to indicate that trial lawyers indeed are a shoddy bunch. Fortunately, that is not wholly true, but looking for a shoddy lawyer is not like looking for a needle in a haystack. Arthur H. Garwin, Counsel for the ABA Center for Professional Responsibility, wrote that "disciplinary rules and the contempt powers of courts provide avenues for dealing with lawyers who overstep the bounds of zealous advocacy."[262] True, but a little bit misleading. According to Professor McElhaney, "most of the lawyers I know are honest and ethical, keep their word and do their best to play by the rules."[263] Surely, he is not talking about the Rules that allow shenanigans. Perhaps lawyers would gain by keeping in mind one of George Washington's Rules of Civility. "Labour to keep alive in your breast that little spark of celestial fire called conscience."[264]

---

258. Lawyer, November 1995, p. 21
259. Landsman, p. 55
260. *Newsweek*, September 28, 1998, p. 42
261. Landsman, p. 211
262. Journal, June 1995, p. 101
263. Journal, May 2004, p. 31
264. Brookhiser, p. 88

Judge Horn seems to have hit the nail squarely on the head when he concluded that "we may need to engage in some hard, clear thinking about whether new boundaries to, 'zealous advocacy' should be fashioned and constructed."[265]

Dean Daisy Floyd of Mercer University School of Law in Macon, Georgia, believes that "what most clients really want from their lawyers [is to] move through the conflict without losing their integrity, their values, their identity."[266] Presumably, she is thinking of civil suits, not criminal suits.

One more disturbing thought along this line. Under the caption, *May vs. Must* "Ethics Rules Don't Give Layers Absolute Guidance on When to Report Wrongdoing," lawyer Kathleen Maher, with the ABA Center for Professional Responsibility, wrote the following.

> Finding the exact boundaries of the ethical obligation to report wrongdoing by others can be a great source of turmoil. What often makes the decision difficult is that a lawyer must reconcile the obligation to report wrongdoing with duties to preserve client confidences.
>
> As a result, the ethics rules don't always offer absolute guidance to a lawyer trying to decide whether to report wrongdoing by a client, another lawyer or a judge, or even someone not involved in a case. While the rules generally permit lawyers to report wrongdoing, they don't always require it.[267]

Lawyer Kagan perhaps sums up this situation when he wrote the following in his book, *Adversarial Legalism*.

> American lawyers and law professors, in sharp contrast to their counterparts in other democratic nations, have created and defended a body of legal ethics that exalts adversarial legalism. In the United States (far more than elsewhere) lawyers' codes of ethics endorse zealous advocacy of clients' causes, short of dishonesty, but without regard to the interests of justice in the particular case or broader societal concerns. American lawyers' professional culture is unique in permitting and implicitly encouraging them to advance unprecedented legal claims, coach witnesses, and attempt to wear down their opponents through burdensome pretrial discovery. In the hands of

---

265. Horn, p. 50
266. Journal, January 2005, p. 76
267. Journal, November 2005, p. 30

some practitioners—not all, but not merely a few—entrepreneurial, manipulative, and super aggressive modes of getting clients and litigating push the limits of adversarial legalism even further.

Perhaps most important, American law professors, judges, and lawyers have elaborated legal theories that actively promote adversarial legalism not as a necessary evil but as a desirable mode of governance. Their heroic view of the judiciary's role in government...has not been uncontested in the law schools or in the judiciary.[268]

PROFESSIONALISM VS. OFFICERS OF THE COURT:

THE ETHICS NON-SOLUTION

Lawyer Katz sounds as if she is discouraged by the antics of the legal profession, although she does not entirely blame the individual lawyer.

Confusion is inherent in the profession. An attorney is obligated, professionally and morally, to champion his or her client's cause. But an attorney is also an 'officer of the court,' exercising powers such as subpoena on behalf of society as a whole. And, increasingly, attorneys are also businesspeople with personal interests in outcomes...The vast majority of attorneys probably balance these conflicting forces ethically. However, the growing popular perception, and the increasing sense of not a few lawyers, is that the profession is no longer honorable.

Today, lawyers are actually obliged to obfuscate and distort the truth or else risk the penalties of malpractice or professional censure....[The system] allows no substitute for winning for one's client; the other guy is the enemy....The reality in the courtroom is that you cannot admit that the other side has a point.

Since the bottom line of lawyering cannot be truth and justice, it must be bottom-line moneymaking....It bothers the young lawyer for a while, but it becomes easier—like a lie: difficult at first, but with practice you hardly notice it.[269]

Lawyer Crier is perhaps more direct.

---

268. Kagan, pp. 55,56
269. Katz, pp. 43,44

To enterprising attorneys, there are few unmerited lawsuits. Traditionally, lawyers were officers of the court who zealously represented clients within legal and ethical boundaries. The interests of justice were paramount, such that intentionally misleading a jury or using discovery simply to wear down an opponent or drain his pocketbook was degrading to the practitioner and unethical as well. Using court pleadings or the media as a litigation tactic to destroy an opponent was unacceptable. Attorneys now regularly solicit clients, conjure up creative and nuisance filings, and delay the trial process, all to line their own pockets.[270]

As you read this chapter, keep in mind the conflicting rules of the *ABA Model Rules*. For instance, "A lawyer, as a member of the legal profession, is a representative of clients, an officer of the legal system and a public citizen having special responsibility for the quality of justice."[271] Compare that to "As advocate, a lawyer zealously asserts the client's position under the rules of the adversary system.... A lawyer should keep in confidence information relating to representation of a client"[272]

These conflicting, rule dictates are not compatible, at least in practice. Consider them under our adversarial system. Which comes first, the lawyer serving as an officer of the court or the lawyer as zealous advocate of the client? It is not possible to do both equally. As a result, the lawyer as an officer of the court takes a distant back seat to zealous representation. According to Richard L. Abel, Professor at the University of California School of Law, Los Angeles, some critics claim that "ethical rules were motivated by economic self-interest."[273] This may be the problem.

New York lawyer Charles Rembar, now deceased, possibly would have agreed, even though what he said is somewhat mind-boggling even for those who disagree with the adversarial system.

> Lawyers in litigation should be paid not by their clients but by the government. Lawyers are theoretically officers of the court, and their services in our adversary system are as much a part of the attempt to achieve justice as the services of judges, clerks and bailiffs. The theory

---

270. Crier, p. 188
271. Rules, p. 1
272. Rules, p. 1
273. Abel, p. 17

should be given real effect, and lawyers should get their compensation from the judicial institution rather than from those who find the need to use it.[274]

In discussing self-regulation of the profession, Professor Abel pointed out that "one of the hallmarks that distinguishes a profession from other occupations is the power and practice of self-regulation."[275] But he then continues, "The suspicion that professional associations promulgate ethical rules more to legitimate themselves in the eyes of the public than to engage in effective regulation is strengthened by the inadequacy of enforcement mechanisms...ethical rules are not self-enforcing. Surveys repeatedly show that lawyers are ignorant of many rules and fail to internalize those they do know."[276] Professor Abel was not done with chastising the professions.

> If structural functionalism had to distinguish professions by means of a single characteristic, self-regulation would be a prime candidate.... Professions are adamant that they, not the state or the consumer, must exercise regulatory authority.... Professions rest their argument for self-regulation on two grounds. First, they insist that only fellow professionals possess the necessary expertise to judge professional performance. Even if true, this is self-serving, since the profession deliberately constructed the monopoly of expertise in the first place. Second, they point to the profession's independence from the state; but this assumes that the profession is more solicitous than the state or client (and other public) interests and will defend those interests against the state—empirical propositions for which there is little evidence.[277]

As stated previously, confusion exists in the legal field. What is said and what is done barely show a relationship to each other. This is not unusual in the political arena, but it should not exist in a profession, particularly in the legal profession. The ABA's Commission on Professionalism idealized that "the lawyer has an obligation to the legal system in his capacity as an officer of the court to dissuade the client from pursuing matters that should not be in

---

274. Rembar, p. 40
275. Abel, p. 142
276. Abel, p. 143
277. Abel, p. 37

court in the first place, and from using tactics geared primarily to drain the financial resources of the other side."[278]

Again, idealistically, as long ago as 1958, the ABA and the Association of American Law Schools jointly determined that the lawyer's role was to forestall litigation by "anticipating its outcome...the lawyer's quiet counsel [to take] the place of public force."[279] Professor Rhode would probably agree since she is a critic of that adversarial ideology that says the "lawyers' undivided client allegiance serves fundamental interests of individual dignity, privacy, and autonomy."[280]

She further states that "professional ideology has become detached from society's more general ethical norms. Relieved of any responsibility for substantive justice, lawyers can come to view it as peripheral to their own sense of achievement. Litigation becomes a game or ritual...such perspectives relieve the process of any necessity to generate fair or rational results." She then quotes a British barrister who said, "I have seldom felt better pleased than when I persuaded [the court] to come to a decision which I was convinced was wrong"[281] Instead of pleased, shouldn't he have felt guilty? To be a good trial lawyer, apparently one of the requisites is to be bereft of a conscience.

Perhaps so, since Professor Hazard once wrote this. "Legitimate and illegitimate techniques shade into each other—vigorous maneuver into harassment, careful preparation of witnesses into subornation of perjury, nondisclosure into destruction of evidence. At some point in deterioration of rules of form, an expert in rough and tumble becomes simply a thug."[282] Professor Rhode would agree. "To assume that clients are entitled to assistance in any action not plainly prohibited collapses moral and legal rights."[283]

---

278. Abel, p. 243
279. Landsman, p. 180
280. Landsman, p. 191
281. Landsman, p. 191
282. Landsman, p. 202
283. Landsman, p. 192

Professor Freedman, plainly of a different stripe, would not agree. "The attorney's obligation of entire devotion to the interests of the client, and warm zeal in the maintenance and defense of the client's rights, would seem to be beyond serious controversy."[284]

Preceding our present legal system, "ethical rules [were] set up to control the legal profession itself. Yesterday's lawyers were specifically forbidden to 'stir up litigation.' Unlike ordinary tradesmen they were expected to sit passively waiting for clients, smothering any entrepreneurial urge they might feel to drum up business."[285] Unfortunately, that is not true today. "Honor, fidelity, fairness, and duty are replaced by the interests of fame, fortune, and public spectacle."[286] Former Chief Justice Warren Burger, obviously relying on lawyers' skills rather than their honesty, opined that it "is the lawyer's responsibility to recognize the evasion and to bring the witness back to the mark, to flush out the whole truth with the tools of adversary examination."[287]

The goal of ruthless cross-examination, however, is not primarily to establish the truth. It is to win the lawsuit. St. Louis lawyer Rex Carr was quoted as saying "to me, the trial of lawsuits is the *summum bonum* of this business. This is an arena. It's combat. Me against the other lawyers. I want to win."[288] That is no surprise to trial lawyers. They must be ruthless in all aspects of the judicial system in order to expect victory. "The accepted rule in litigation is that a lawyer cannot afford to play nicer than the most un-nice lawyer in the case."[289]

Apparently in the minority, lawyer Ken Starr, famous for his relentless, but fruitless, pursuit of President Clinton, stated that "the search for the truth, not the service of the client, is the legal system's abiding value."[290] Islands of hope for a decent judicial

---

284. Landsman, p. 198
285. Olson, p. 3
286. Rothwax, p. 129
287. Bronston v. U.S., 409 U.S. 352, (1973)
288. Jenkins, p. 372
289. Olson, p. 232
290. *Newsweek*, September 28, 1998, p. 42

system, though rather minuscule, do exist. Judge Aspen once wrote that "any notion that the duty to represent a client trumps obligations of professionalism is, of course, indefensible as a matter of law."[291]

According to Professor Braithwaite, "professionalism seems to be the fashionable word for what used to be called character.... However defined, professionalism is a kind of excellence or, a word no longer fashionable, virtue."[292] In spite of the niceties of professionalism, "legal practice has gotten more ferociously adversarial,"[293] even though lawyers are still considered officers of the court. As long as we have the adversarial system, one must be resigned to the fact that the system is incompatible to true professionalism.

Possibly without much hope for success, Judge Horn lists what a lawyer should be in order to be truly recognized as an officer of the court.

> First, that law can and should be understood and practiced as something higher and nobler than just a way to make a good living...Second, that we should reconnect with the tradition Elihu Root and others represented: the *counselor* at law. "About half the practice of a decent lawyer," Root once observed, "consists in telling would be clients they are damned fools and should stop." True then, true now. Third, that as "officers of the court" lawyers should embrace ethics, principles, and values far exceeding the *de minimus* requirements of the various Codes of Professional Responsibility. Fourth, that lawyers should look for creative ways to make peace between potential disputants and provide more proactive counsel, regarding litigation as a last resort. And fifth, that the legal profession, from law school through retirement, should embrace balance and wholeness for the professional and personal life of every lawyer.[294]

Hope always springs eternal. Michael Greco, president-elect of the ABA, before taking office in year 2005, said that "he will be talking about the concept of a renaissance of idealism in the profession...lawyers feel 'a malaise and disenchantment, buffeted by

291. Journal, July 1997, p. 95
292. Journal, September 1990, p. 70
293. Journal, October 1991, p. 70
294. Horn, p. 153

economic pressures and federal agencies that want them to snitch on clients.'"[295] It has been interesting to observe how deep he delved into the causes of lawyers' feelings.

THE LAWYER'S IMAGE

"The bar has always suffered from a certain degree of unpopularity."[296] "I think lawyers are thought of now just as they have always been thought of, and that's not very highly."[297] In a Gallop poll conducted November 22-24, 2002, only 18% rated lawyers' honesty and integrity as "high" or "very high."[298] The poor reputation of lawyers is not new. Abe Lincoln once commented that, "There is a vague popular belief that lawyers are necessarily dishonest."[299] Judge Horn believes (as does this writer) that litigation "is probably more responsible for the negative public opinion of lawyers than any other single factor."[300] He further states that "as cynicism about the higher purposes of law—and *the idea* in some quarters that making money is sufficient *raison d'etre* for the profession—have taken hold, public approval and lawyer happiness appear to have fallen."[301]

Lawyer Roger Stone of Cedar Rapids would not quite agree with all that said above.

> The reputation that trial lawyers have is due in large part to a rather concerted publicity attack by the insurance industry and other groups that are involved in defending claims.... But everyone deserves a champion.[302]

---

295. Journal, April 2004, p. 69
296. Friedman(2), p. 303
297. Journal, December 1992, p. 72
298. Iowa State Bar Association Report, Issue 5, December 16, 2002, p. 1
299. Journal, October 1990, p. 98
300. Horn, p. 138
301. Horn, p. 78
302. Gazette, October 7, 2004, p. 10A

Individual clients generally seem to like their own attorneys, but what the public sees is something different. Perhaps Justice David B. Saxe of the New York State Supreme Court got it right.

> The lawyers that the public probably sees are the trial lawyers. They're the most visible lawyers—and they are arrogant.... They're actors; they're performers. Performers are full of themselves and are arrogant. They are people who are ultimately not the most sensitive of individuals. They have huge egos. And those are the kinds of people upon which the public bases its perception.[303]

Professor Abel has a good slant on the legal profession.

> Lawyers constantly bemoan the fact that they are misunderstood and undervalued. But they will never increase public respect through conspicuous acts of altruism or sporadic crackdowns on ambulance chasing. People are not fools; lawyers must change who they are and what they do if they want to change how they are perceived.... Instead of seeking to justify their actions by reference to process values that allegedly produce truth and justice, lawyers must concede—indeed, affirm—that they actively promote the objectives of their clients and justify their own behavior in terms of the substantive justice of their clients' goals.[304]

Inherent in the word "behavior" is our adversarial system of justice and the manner in which trial lawyers abuse the system on behalf of their clients. Although adversaryism itself is inherently bad, the trial lawyers' corruption of it has destroyed their reputation. Judge Scieszinksi believes that "lawyers must extract their egos from their work, and avoid the temptation to internalize the quested 'win,' thus obscuring the real merits of the case and overlooking practical alternatives for addressing them."[305]

Iowa Supreme Court Justice Mark S. Cady believes that "conduct in a professional capacity may be acceptable when judged by legal standards, yet offensive to people outside the legal profession, or other lawyers within the profession, when judged by their personal ethics."[306]

---

303. Journal, November 1992, p. 74
304. Abel, p. 247
305. Journal, June 1995, p. 119
306. Lawyer, May 1992, p. 9

Robert J. Samuelson, contributing editor of *Newsweek* and columnist for the *Washington Post*, an admitted "lawyer-basher" although a trained lawyer himself, believes that what's wrong with lawyers "is that they have an economic interest in cultivating and prolonging conflict."[307] Unfortunately, Samuelson paints lawyers with too broad a brush, since most lawyers are not trial lawyers. In fact, if the truth were known, it is doubtful that most lawyers even enjoy conflict. Judge Scieszinski makes an observation, which probably explains why Samuelson could be confused. "Lawyers in the courtrooms command the headlines, not those in the trenches solving problems without fanfare."[308]

Both Barry Melton, a San Francisco public defender lawyer, and Becky Klemt, a Laramie, Wyoming, lawyer, believe that many lawyers are not happy in their profession.[309] District Judge J. Michael Coffey of Omaha believes that "the negative image of lawyers has resulted from the adversarial nature of our profession."[310] It is not far-fetched to believe that the negative feelings of many lawyers is related to the judicial system under which they must operate. Consider that many lawyers, who no doubt felt good about themselves before entering the practice, are no longer content after discovering the manner in which many trials are conducted.

It is difficult to gauge whether bar leaders who speak in generalities about professionalism and civility are speaking from the heart or only mimicking what they believe the public wants to hear. Judge Horn, however, says that "whether or not it is entirely deserved, the general public's low opinion of lawyers must be acknowledged and engaged."[311]

---

307. *Newsweek*, April 27, 1992, p. 62
308. Journal, June 1995, p. 119
309. Journal, December 1992, pp. 70,71
310. Journal, January 1989, p. 12
311. Horn, p. 2

The Attorney-Client Relationship and Privileges

In a nutshell, the attorney-client privilege refers to what a client tells or reveals to his or her attorney. Whatever the information, it is a secret as between the two of them unless its revelation is consented to by the client or is for the client's benefit. The general rule is that the privilege is imposed even though such secrecy could do harm to a third party or society in general. However some cracks in the rule have appeared, principally resulting from corporate malfeasance.[312] According to former ABA President R. William Ide III, the attorney-client privilege "is a very hot issue within the profession."[313]

Although the attorney-client relationship is addressed by the *ABA Model Rules*,[314] these Rules merely reflect the long-standing practice of confidentiality held by the attorney to the client. According to Professor Landsman, adoption of the attorney-client privilege occurred around 1577. "Lawyers were granted a special exemption from the obligation to provide evidence if it was originally provided to them by their clients. Although the privilege was first premised upon the dignity of the attorney, the rule clearly facilitated the lawyer's freewheeling search for evidence by insulating him from compulsion to disclose information obtained from his client."[315]

Observe the following statement made in the *ABA Journal* during a discussion as to what the public thinks of lawyers. "It is likely that the public views as unethical any defense attorney who would keep silent about a client who confessed a murder to him or her. Yet lawyers know that without the attorney-client privilege in such instances, effective defense would be virtually impossible."[316]

---

312. http://www.abanet.org/journal/ereport/m3lethics.html, March 31, 2006, vol. 5, issue 13
313. ABA Journal eReport, February 11, 2005, p. 1
314. Rules, p. 22
315. Landsman, p. 11
316. Journal, September 1993, p. 63

This reveals the twisted logic of the legal profession, or at least of some of its leaders. Defend your clients at all costs. It doesn't matter whether the clients are guilty or innocent. Work to get them a verdict of innocence regardless of the client's guilt and regardless of the harm to society. Nothing matters but the client. Not even the reputation of the legal profession. Under such circumstances, trial lawyers believe that "defend" is synonymous with "representation."

In defense of their conduct, trial lawyers will of course cite the *Model Rules*, which state (more than once) that "a lawyer shall not reveal information relating to the representation of a client unless the client gives informed consent," citing it as a "fundamental principle."[317] Here is what Marianne M. Jennings, Professor of Legal and Ethical Studies, Arizona State University, has to say about codes and their use. "As an ethics professor, I have also found that those who rely most on written codes of conduct are the most unethical among us. They want a fancy document certifying their integrity that they can wave around, but they do not want to be bound by it."[318]

In discussing self-regulation by professions, Professor Abel stated that "client confidentiality is invoked to obstruct external surveillance of professional misconduct."[319] Compare that to what Professor Alschuler says. "The [legal] system becomes substantially more just when a client can rely on his attorney without question or doubt—when he can know as well as he is likely ever to know the future that giving the truth to his attorney will not hurt him."[320] Judge Rothwax had a different slant. "While it is true that defense attorneys have a primary loyalty to their clients, they can't simply ignore ethics and decency in the process. Good lawyers should not be bad citizens."[321]

Lawyer Elderkin once correctly stated that the standards of professional conduct "do not require the lawyer to judge the

---

317. Rules, p.22
318. Imprimus, July 1999, Volume 28, Number 7, p. 3
319. Abel, p. 38
320. Landsman, p. 210
321. Rothwax, p. 226

'morality' of the client's cause"[322] The joint conference of the ABA and the Association of American Law Schools held in 1958, while recognizing that the attorney should be a zealous advocate, was concerned that the profession should "perceive truly the limits partisan advocacy must impose on itself if it is to remain wholesome and useful."[323] As indicated by Elderkin's statement, that concern died in its infancy.

Much later, in 1995, an article in *Newsweek* stated it thus. "The basic rule now is to represent your client as zealously as possible. Lawyers rarely feel a conflict between representing their clients and acting as an 'officer of the court.'"[324] In other words, confessions of clients to their lawyers do not detract or derail their attorneys from a vigorous defense, a defense that assumes, actually claims, the innocence of the client. The purpose of this stance by the defense attorney is, of course, not to educe the truth of the charges but rather to gain a verdict of not guilty.

Professor Freedman is not bothered by the moral dilemma sometimes imposed upon a lawyer in abiding by the attorney-client relationship. He speaks of the "obligation of the lawyers to their client and, in a larger sense, to a system of administering justice which is itself essential to maintaining human dignity."[325] In this instance, Professor Freedman speaks approvingly of the lawyer who did not reveal the location of two bodies that had been murdered and buried by his client. The word "dignity" often appears in statements by those who approve the adversarial system and the attorney-client relationship. This surely is a mere pretense to justify their position. Hopefully, they don't really believe that lawyers and their clients who hide the truth, lie, cheat, and otherwise defraud the court have any dignity, regardless of their motives. Professor Alschuler would disagree since he believes that "the lawyer's basic

---

322. Lawyer, November 1995, p. 21
323. Landsman, p. 179
324. *Newsweek*, March 20, 1995, p. 36
325. Landsman, p. 184

function is to serve his client's interests, not retard them"[326] Judge Rothwax described it this way.

> The defense lawyer's only goal is to represent his client with zeal, within the bounds of law. He's not interested in society. He's not interested in the victim. His client, the defendant, is entitled to a champion. And his lawyer will perform that function in every way possible within the limits of the law.[327]

In this instance, Judge Rothwax made no explanation of "bounds" or "limits" of the law. Perhaps, as a practical matter, there are none.

Rule 3.3 of the *ABA Model Rules, Candor toward the Tribunal* has been referred to previously.[328] It places a burden upon the trial attorney to be open to the court. Because it requires knowledge of the attorney to do or not to do certain things, the Rule is mostly ignored and unenforceable. And one provision, "A lawyer may [note not "shall"] refuse to offer evidence, other than the testimony of a defendant in a criminal matter, that the lawyer reasonably believes is false,"[329] has a nice loophole tune to it.

Rambo-type trial lawyers "argue that the duty to represent a client zealously is paramount to the administration of justice, even when it conflicts with any obligations of professionalism."[330] This attitude is indefensible, yet not rare. When defending a client, Alan M. Dershowitz, Professor of Law, Harvard Law School, feels obligated to allow his clients to plead not guilty, whatever their guilt. "I'm just their representative, not their conscience. I would never do many of the things in my personal life that I have to do as a lawyer."[331] Now isn't that reassuring.

Perhaps in defense of lawyers, writer Olson wrote that "much of the ethical tension in lawyering is between the obligation to provide effective advocacy for the client and the obligation to

---

326. Landsman, p. 211
327. Rothwax, p. 178
328. See footnote 46
329. Rules, par. 3.3(a)(3), p. 76
330. Journal, July 1997, p. 95
331. Journal, May 1995, p. 39

behave as an 'officer of the court,'" which Olson describes as "a quaint phrase that sums up many ways lawyers are supposed to hold in check their urge to win at all costs."[332]

When Keith McKinley was 1993-1994 President of the Iowa State Bar Association, he spoke about the lawyer's conflict between zealous advocacy and ethics in an address to a first year class at Drake University Law School, Des Moines.

> "When you take your oath as a lawyer you will become an officer of the court. As such you have an obligation to maintain the respect due to the courts and its judicial officers. You are not to counsel or maintain any action, proceeding or defense other than those which appear legal and just, except the defense of a person charged with a public offense.

> "You are further obligated to employ such means only as are consistent with truth, and never to seek to mislead the judges by an artifice or false statement of fact or law.

> "As an advocate you will maintain inviolate the confidence, and, at any peril to yourself, preserve the secret of a client.... Iowa, by the way is one of the few states where violation of an Ethical Consideration is grounds for disciplinary action.

> ".... the practice of law will require you to balance your roles as an officer of the court, as a zealous advocate and as someone who after all is trying to make a living. . . . It is balancing those (first) two that will give you the problem.

> "As an officer of the court truthfulness is your paramount consideration. As an advocate the secret of your client is your paramount consideration... but as between the two, truth is the most important even if it means your withdrawal from representation."[333]

Professor Landsman acknowledged the conflict. "On the one hand, attorneys were expected to be officers of the court and to seek the truth. On the other, they were expected to be keen advocates on behalf of their clients."[334] Unfortunately, in these later years, emphasis has been on the latter, which makes a mockery of the

---

332. Olson, p. 225
333. Lawyer, January 1994, p. 4
334. Landsman, p. 18

former. Not always, though, is the emphasis misplaced. Justice Cady once made the following comments.

> A litigator cannot use the threat of malpractice to excuse conduct which is antagonistic to personal values of common courtesies. Lawyers do not breach their duty to their client, for example, by informing opposing counsel of an oversight or mistake in civil cases, or advising counsel that they are in default prior to moving for default judgment.... It is simply courtesy, compatible with the underlying goal of justice. Advocacy [did he mean adversarial conduct?] is an important part of our legal system, but justice is the goal. Advocacy is simply the chosen means to achieve the goal, not an end in itself. Justice can never be assured in a system lacking individual values.[335]

While discussing the bar's jealous control of the attorney-client relationship, Professor Rhode speaks of the bar's inconsistency when secrecy causes personal harm.

> It bears note that even the most fervent defenders of unqualified confidentiality have seldom pursued the logic of their position when attorneys' own interests are at issue. Few...Rules evoke greater consensus than the provision allowing lawyers to reveal information necessary to collect fees or to establish their own position in a dispute with the client. Yet nothing...explains why disclosures to protect lay victims will erode client trust, while revelations to secure attorneys' financial interests will not. In effect, the bar's selective endorsement of confidentiality exceptions concedes the empirical point at issue. Once one acknowledges that clients' general expectation of confidentiality can be maintained despite some limited risk of betrayal, it is unclear why the pecuniary concerns of lawyers should assume priority over the potentially more significant claims of third-party victims. In short, the profession is scarcely well situated to make a disinterested assessment of the societal risks and benefits of less categorical confidentiality protections.[336]

The confidentiality rule is of long-standing, although that in and of itself does not justify its existence. It is an arbitrary rule that has no justification in contested matters. Defense counsel should make as certain as possible, indeed they have the duty to determine, that their clients receive decent treatment and a fair, meaning an honest, truthful result. The trial court should not ordinarily be the

---

335. Lawyer, May 1992, p. 11
336. Landsman, p. 214

forum for this to occur. Contrary to admirers of the US system, court trials under this system do not guarantee that results are fair or even correct. Moreover, courts should not be cluttered with disputes that result from clandestine communications between lawyer and client.

The goal of trial lawyers should not be to win, but rather to make certain that both parties receive exactly what they deserve. Satisfaction should come from knowing that the end result is fitting for their client, even though their client is convicted or held liable. If clients are not liable or guilty as alleged, then no earthly reason exists for the keeping of their secrets. On the other hand, if clients are in fact liable or guilty as alleged, then keeping their secrets is in direct conflict with the interests of a civilized society.

The British system not only should be envied, it should be emulated. "Barristers owe their primary duty to the court and not to the client."[337] In other words, the barrister represents, but does not defend, the client who is in fact guilty or liable.

Again, hope is on the horizon. For the last twenty years, New Jersey lawyer Edwin Stier "has advised [corporate] clients to waive privilege to prove they are sincere when they say they want to root out problems, no matter what an independent investigation reveals."[338] Some lawyers have a contrary thought. "Securities lawyer Michael L. Jamieson, who heads Holland & Knight's corporate governance group in Tampa, Fla., shares the pervasive view that tinkering with attorney-client privilege is a dangerous trend. He argues that pressuring clients to waive privilege is likely to make clients less candid if they believe their lawyers will turn into agents of the government."[339] One cannot help but assume that if a client is not candid, then that client has something to hide.

Unfortunately, 2004 ABA President Dennis W. Archer seems to agree with Jamieson. "We have worked with the Securities and Exchange Commission...to assure that the new rules preserve the

---

337. Journal, January 1991, p. 62
338. Journal, May 2004, p. 24
339. Journal, May 2004, p. 24

ability of lawyers to advise corporate clients on compliance with the law and to represent them vigorously and professionally. One of the ABA's highest priorities is to protect attorney-client privilege, certainly a bedrock principle of the profession."[340]

In the past, President Archer did not sound quite that adamant. In August 2003, the ABA's policy-making House of Delegates revised Model Rule 1.6: Confidentiality of Information, to permit "a lawyer to reveal information relating to the representation of a client to the extent the lawyer believes necessary to prevent the client from committing a crime or fraud that would lead to 'substantial injury to the financial interests or property of another and in furtherance of which the client has used or is using the lawyer's services.'" Prior to its passage and during its debate, then incoming President Archer "said the rule revision would not undermine the 'core values' of the legal profession because it is 'talking about a client who uses you or attempts to use you as an accomplice in his dirty work.'"[341]

Possibly because "the lawyer-client relationship [is] increasingly stressful and problematic,"[342] "the nature of attorney-client relationship is changing."[343] A "new" ABA ethics standard allows "lawyers to reveal client confidences to prevent crimes or frauds resulting in financial losses."[344] And, of course, lawyers can always reveal confidences if the purpose is to protect their own skin.

Perceived Ills

America's adversarial judicial system has many ills, most of which probably can be attributed to its contentious characteristics, a form of judicial procedure that incites rather than mollifies the participants. No doubt, many laypersons believe this is why lawyers tout the adversarial form: to create and perpetuate litigation. This form of justice seems to breed problems, to bring out the worse in those who would be the black sheep in any endeavor. Conceivably,

---

340. ABAMembership@ABANET.ORG, 3-25-04 10:01 AM, p. 1, to members
341. Journal, October 2003, p. 80
342. Horn, p. 108
343. ISBA e-mail, October 7, 2004, p. 1
344. Journal, October 2003, p. 80

it is our form of adversarial justice that encourages wrongdoing. Mere lip service to true justice cannot control the system, when truth is so easily manipulated and disregarded.

Consider our much maligned tort system. One of its criticisms is that "it provides opportunity for costly, groundless suits—the lawyers gamble that they might win big awards...the contingent-fee system permits over-reaching by lawyers, to the disadvantage of inexperienced claimants, at a time when clients are least able to negotiate a better fee arrangement."[345] In a few instances, limits have been placed on the amount of fees, but that only indicates that a problem may exist. The elimination of the adversarial system would be a much better solution to the faults of the tort system than controlling fees.

Adversaryism allows for a wide-open trial system. Depending upon financial resources, parties can utilize a "war of attrition...they make the litigation as financially and economically burdensome as possible...they use whatever procedural tactics they can employ...they do a lot of clever lawyering...they divert your attention from the main issues."[346] Imagine the satisfaction to all except a few trial attorneys if the adversarial system did not exist.

Thoroughly frustrated, Judge Rothwax had this to say about the unbecoming conduct of trial lawyers. "With the intention of being overruled, a defense attorney will often seek to 'seed the record' with error. Issues will be raised for no other purpose than to provoke error...Although our professional ethics would seem to forbid such behavior, there is no bright line between acceptable courtroom gamesmanship and misbehavior."[347]

Cessation of the adversarial system would help to eliminate this kind of unprofessional behavior. But it will be difficult. Consider what lawyer Kagan wrote.

> American lawyers—unlike British barristers and European lawyers—are trained to believe that their primary responsibility is not to uncover the truth and produce the "correct" legal disposition but to

345. Journal, November 1, 1988, p. 36
346. Jenkins, p. 159
347. Rothwax, p. 135

get the best possible result for their clients. They also can be counted on to mount intense political resistance to any proposed legal changes that would sharply diminish their abilities to do so.[348]

The ABA Rules specify what constitutes misconduct of a lawyer. For instance, it is unprofessional for a lawyer to "engage in conduct that is prejudicial to the administration of justice."[349] In spite of such rules, many judges report that "more lawyers appearing before them are bending the truth, not telling the whole truth or just plain lying about everything from discovery to the holdings of prior decisions."[350]

Professor Erwin Chemerinsky of USC Law School seems to be straddling the fence when he says "I don't think it's the lawyer's duty to push the client for the truth, but the lawyer shouldn't vouch so strongly for the client either."[351] Trial lawyers who favor adversaryism maintain that it is the opposing attorney's duty to wring the truth out of the other attorney's client. However, isn't that an appalling time to find out the truth, if ever? Think of the time it takes to even arrive at trial and yet it is only then, hopefully, that the truth can be determined. In addition, the adversarial system does not guarantee that truth will come out even at that late date. It would be much better if every officer of the court attempted to find the truth as soon as possible, especially prior to trial or, even better yet, prior to filing suit.

Professor Landsman, in detailing the history of the practice of law, said that "as proceedings became more adversarial, conflicting ethical demands were exerted upon lawyers.... On the one hand, attorneys were expected to be officers of the court and to seek the truth. On the other, they were expected to be keen advocates on behalf of their clients."[352] Encouraged by greed and the *Model Rules*, the emphasis has been on the latter, which makes a mockery of the former. If truth, rather than winning, were sought, then truth is suf-

---

348. Kagan, p. 244
349. Rules, p. 120
350. Journal, May 1995, p. 70
351. Journal, December 1998, p. 54
352. Landsman, p. 18

ficient to protect the honest client. Dishonest clients are not entitled to the quirky protection that the adversarial system gives them.

Professor Landsman had more to say.

> The adversary system is based upon the premise that each litigant will forcefully and completely present his or her case...the primary function of lawyers in such a system is to speak for those who employ them...advocates [see] themselves as more than mere mouthpieces for hire. They have recognized that the nature of their work creates special obligations to the legal system they work in and the society that supports it. How to balance allegiance to clients and society has been a matter of constant debate.[353]

If a client is honorable, why should there be any debate? If a client is honorable, allegiance to society will not harm the client. But if a client is not honorable, why give him or her opportunity via the adversary system to harm society or any member thereof?

Lawyer Rembar rebuked lawyers in a different way. "The premise [is] that lawyers are more reprehensible than other people who work for a living. The premise is wrong. Lawyers in general behave slightly better than most occupational groups. There is another judgmental basis, however, which is valid: slightly better is not enough. A profession that concerns itself with law and justice should be considerably better than most."[354]

During the O. J. Simpson era, lawyer Rosenberg made the following observation.

> Most people do not understand the adversary system. Or at least they do not understand that, within certain ethical boundaries, lawyers are permitted or even required to advance arguments for their clients even though the arguments may be less than fully persuasive. Indeed, many people seem to view the justice system as a pristine search for truth, where lawyers on both sides ought to serve as assistant truth-seekers. Many people's comments appear to suggest that they would be more comfortable, at least in theory, with an inquisitorial system based on the European model. [They further believe that] lawyers should be punished for 'bad' behavior in trials.[355]

---

353. Landsman, p. 170
354. Rembar, p. 266
355. Journal, June 1995, pp. 74,76

If Rosenberg's perception of the public mood is correct, then the bar should not be reluctant to discard the adversarial system. But if it is, then maybe the bar itself is actually afraid of truth. Is this why a "substantial minority" of lawyers are "miserable," "unhappy," or "lonely, painfully lonely"?[356]

PROSECUTORS VS. DEFENSE ATTORNEYS

While President of the Oregon District Attorney's Associ-ation, Clatsop County, Oregon, District Attorney Joshua Marquis' hackles were raised when it was suggested that persons presented to a grand jury for possible criminal prosecution be therein repre-sented by criminal defense lawyers. In retort, Marquis said that "we have entirely different ethical rules. Our job is to prosecute only people who did it, i.e. guilty defendants, and a defense lawyer's job is to extricate almost always factually guilty clients from any responsi-bility for their acts."[357]

Although this argument pertained to the grand jury system, it rather illuminates the difference between prosecutors and defense attorneys. Ethical rules, actually ethical behavior, are not the same for both. Whereas one is trying to prove the truth of the allegations, the other is trying to hide the truth by avoiding it or by mangling it. Though this behavior by a defense attorney may not be considered ethical, yet it is quite acceptable, possible, and not uncommon under the adversarial system. Moreover, it is not a crime to so behave, although it smacks of being a conspiracy to evade the law.

Consider the following contention, which should be con-sidered unethical but is not under the Rules. Tamara Rice Lave, a public defender in Vista, California, stated that "it doesn't matter to me whether my client really committed a crime. My job is to advocate, and that means I must present the evidence in the way

---

356. Horn, p. 23
357. Journal, March 2001, p. 11

most beneficial to my client.... My goal is to expose reasonable doubt."[358]

Note that she shows no regard for the truth. It is something else, something apparently beyond her apprehension and those of like mind. Such stance does not enhance the reputation of lawyers in general. If the adversarial system disappeared, so would the disregard for truth.

Lawyer Knight briefly discusses the frequent saying about lawyers. "You guys will represent anybody."[359] Note that Knight used the word "represent," not the word "defend," two entirely different words. Every defendant, whether in a civil or criminal case, is entitled to be, and should be, represented. The connotations of the two words, though, are different. To defend, at least as some trial lawyers now use the term, means that no holds are barred. Everything goes. A lawyer, of course, cannot defend without also representing, but a lawyer can responsibly represent without resorting to the tactics of many defense attorneys. Trial lawyers would improve their stature considerably if they would learn to say "I represent," rather than saying "I am defending."

Judge Rothwax was openly and severely critical of the judicial system, as indicated in the following passage.

> This willingness [of lawyers] to perform adversary stunts runs deeper than greed. It interferes with the very nature of the process. The defense attorney cannot be just a 'mouthpiece,' but neither is he a public servant. He must be permitted and obliged to assert the rights that are available to his client under law. Given the probability that the defendant is guilty, the defense attorney knows that the defendant will win *only* if counsel is successful in *preventing* the truth from being disclosed—or, failing that, misleading the jury once it is disclosed. So, when the defendant is guilty, the defense attorney's role is to prevent, distort, and mislead.[360]

Professor Emeritus Harry L. Subin, New York University School of Law, said this.

---

358. *Newsweek*, July 13, 1998, p. 14
359. Knight, p. 198
360. Rothwax, p. 141

It is time to change ethics rules that allow defense attorneys to throw out false theories as a way to clear their clients. Existing ethics rules are so ambiguous that lawyers can justify most of their actions.... While a defendant should be able to test the strength of the state's evidence, an attorney who knows that facts of the state's case are accurate should not be able to try to convince the jury otherwise.... If a defendant has no defense, he or she should not be allowed to make one up.... I don't think the Constitution requires you to put on a frivolous defense.... Ultimately, the Constitution does not really guarantee a person will be able to get off by clever lawyering.[361]

A *Newsweek* article pointed out that defense lawyers don't really want to hear the truth from their client as it could become a "big nuisance.... Many defense lawyers...have no interest in being priests; they want to get acquittals, not give absolution."[362]

Professor Fuller says that "the function of the advocate...is not to decide but to persuade. He is not expected to present the case in a colorless and detached manner, but in such a way that it will appear in the aspect most favorable to his client."[363]

Zita Weinshienk, Senior US District Court Judge in Denver, does not pick merely on defense attorneys. She says that "prosecutors and defense attorneys have always preyed upon the prejudices of judges and jurors."[364]

Regardless how defense attorneys comport themselves, "every criminal defendant is guaranteed an advocate—a 'champion' against a 'hostile world', the 'single voice on which he must rely with confidence that his interests will be protected to the fullest extent"[365] Unfortunately, however, the following is how we see them.

We see them wrangling and bargaining in and out of court to get the best verdict or the best deal, the slightest edge, for seedy characters who are usually, face it, guilty...We see them performing mostly as specialists in delay and obfuscation: obtaining endless trial postponements, grousing about obviously just rulings and verdicts, threatening to appeal their richly deserved losses.[366]

361. Journal, October 1999, p. 44
362. *Newsweek*, August 1, 1994, p. 22
363. Landsman, p. 47
364. Journal, October 1995, p. 58
365. Landsman, p. 185
366. Knight, p. 214

That is bad enough, but some things are even worse, the way defendants and witnesses are prepared for trial. While it is proper to attempt to refresh the parties' recollections of events, it is not proper to put ideas in their heads or to caution them to "don't volunteer anything...The concern is not that the volunteered contribution may be false. The concern is to avoid an excess of truth, where the spillover may prove hurtful to the case."[367] These are the ordinary steps in the war planning, deemed necessary in the US system of justice.

This system seems to bring out the worse in some lawyers who use the system for their own advantage, not that of society. However, "the bulk of criminal trial lawyers, on both sides, spend the bulk of their time and energies avoiding trials in the bulk of their cases."[368] This could be for a variety of reasons unrelated to the adversarial system, such as time restraints, getting a better deal, and financial resources of the defendant. Writer Post believes that "a good, busy lawyer will try to keep his client out of court,"[369] although, in saying that, he is probably contemplating the civil, rather than the criminal, case.

367. Landsman, p. 57
368. Landsman, p. 59
369. Post, p. 136

CHAPTER 5. LEGAL PROCEDURES

THE PROBLEMS

Judge Neely takes a rather dim view of trials, particularly those involving civil suits, although what he says could also apply to criminal suits.

> In the universe of all the routine cases that go to court, most of the time one party will be flat wrong, and he or she will know that from the beginning.... The egalitarian bias that demands free access to court services is predicated on the assumption, however, that both litigants in all lawsuits have a good-faith dispute. Empirically this is an entirely unfounded assumption. Courts are not primarily in the dispute resolution business; they are really in the business of making the side in the wrong pay up. Enforcement, not conflict resolution, is what courts largely accomplish—but because most ironclad claims still can be disputed one way or another, no matter how frivolously, the court must go through the sham of resolving a so-called dispute before it can make an enforceable award.[370]

A great difference exists, however, between a trial of a civil case and that of a criminal case. Especially in criminal cases, a defendant does not have to admit anything, yet a failure of admission in a criminal case makes it more than likely that the alle-

---

370. Neely, p. 166

gations against a criminal defendant cannot be proven. "In a criminal proceeding, proof of guilt must be 'beyond a reasonable doubt.' In a civil case, proof rests upon a *preponderance of evidence.* This means 'that the party having the burden of proving certain facts must make it appear more probable than not that those facts existed.'"[371] As lawyer Rembar pointed out, "It is a hard fact to face, but perfect protection of the accused means imperfect protection of society"[372]

Writer Post quotes Dean Pound as saying that our procedure is one of "the most efficient causes of dissatisfaction with the present administration of justice in America."[373] Changes have been made in our administration of justice since Dean Pound's speech of 1906 but it is doubtful that Pound ever took back his words. According to E. Allan Farnsworth, Professor of Law, Columbia University School of Law, "Like the rest of the law of procedure, the law of evidence bears the stamp both of the adversary character of litigation and of the institution of the jury. In keeping with the contentious nature of the proceeding, the initiative is on the parties rather than the judge both to develop the evidence and police its admission."[374]

In describing the characteristics of criminal procedure, Professor Farnsworth said that "criminal procedure in America is essentially accusatory, with the prosecutor taking the leading role, rather than inquisitorial, with the judge taking the leading role. The trial of criminal, even more than civil, cases reflects the adversary nature of the judicial process and confidence in the capacities of laymen as jurors."[375] Lawyer Spence describes a trial as "a barbarous sport conducted in accordance with certain civilized rules.... Rarely will the fight be fair. As in most sports, those who can afford the best

---

371. Post, p. 134
372. Rembar, p. 95
373. Post, p. 135
374. Farnsworth, p. 113
375. Farnsworth, p. 109

players generally win."[376] Similarly, former prosecutor Bugliosi described the Simpson trial merely as a "game."[377]

Lawrence M. Friedman, Professor of Law, Stanford Law School, has this disconcerting thought about our judicial system.

> The modern European law of evidence is fairly simple and rational; the law lets most everything in, and trusts the judge to separate good evidence from bad. But American law distrusts the judge; it gives the jury full fact-finding power and, in criminal cases, the final word on innocence or guilt. Yet the law distrusts the jury as much as it distrusts the judge, and the rules of evidence grew up as some sort of countervailing force. The jury only hears part of the story, that part which the law of evidence allows. The judge's hands are also tied. If he lets in improper testimony, he runs the risk that the case will be reversed on appeal. Hence the rules of evidence bind and control both jury and judge.[378]

Relative to criminal trials, Judge Posner gives his insight on the legal system.

> The legal system has erected formidable procedural obstacles to conviction. These have succeeded in reducing the probability of convicting innocent persons to an extremely low level, but the price is that many guilty persons are acquitted (especially those who can afford to hire top-quality lawyers), or are never charged, or are allowed to plead guilty to crimes much less serious than those they actually committed.[379]

As usual, Judge Rothwax was forthright about the importance of truth in the judicial process. "Let us remember that legal procedure is a means, not an end. Therefore, the purpose of procedure should be to enhance the law, not to delay or defeat the law's intention. I believe it stands to reason that a primary objective of procedural rules should be to facilitate the discovery of truth."[380]

Criminal defense attorneys would not agree. For instance, "A defendant will await the filing of an accusation against him before he undertakes to frame an issue to his liking."[381] In other words, the

---

376. Spence, p. 112
377. Bugliosi, p. 15
378. Friedman(2), p. 153
379. Posner, p. 207
380. Rothwax, pp. 31,32

criminal defense attorney will make up a story most suitable for his or her client's defense, the facts be damned. As Judge Rothwax points out, "The defense lawyer's only goal is to represent his client. His only interest is his client—not society, not the victim."[382] The system allows all this, thinks nothing about it. Truth is not important, only the system.

Lawyer Kaminer, perhaps speaking hopefully, said that "a host of rules in criminal cases, regarding admissibility of evidence or qualification of jurors...are designed to ensure what the advocacy system idealizes: a reasonably objective, trustworthy fact-finding process."[383]

Lawyer Rembar explained why the rules exist. "The very fact we are playing a game demands the game have rules."[384] During the O. J. Simpson trial, an *ABA Journal* article had this to say about evidentiary rules. "Much of the public seems to believe the rules of evidence and particularly the squabbles about them, take up needless time. Some have asked, 'Wouldn't it be faster just to let the lawyers ask what they want to ask and witnesses say what they want to say and get on with it?'"[385] Possibly the general public is more perceptive than lawyers.

Harvard professor Dershowitz, one of O. J. Simpson's lawyers, wrote that "the truth is that most criminal defendants are, in fact, guilty."[386] But, according to a *Journal* article, "Cases go to trial, rather than settle out of court, for no other reason than one side is lying and the lie must be exposed."[387] A decision following a trial, however, does not necessarily expose the truth because "a trial is a contest of credibility, [the lawyers' own] and that of their witnesses, with evidence, not truth, at its core...what may or may not have

---

381. Fleming, p. 54. See also, Rothwax, p. 172
382. Rothwax, p. 129
383. Kaminer, p. 78
384. Rembar, p. 322
385. Journal, June 1995, p. 75
386. Journal, September 1996, p. 14
387. Journal, October 1991, p. 69

actually happened...will never objectively be known."[388] This is at least partially explained by Professor Maechling.

> The [trial] process requires the prosecution to present its case in the most awkward way possible—through a succession of witnesses...the last thing a witness is allowed to do is tell his story in his own words and give his opinion of what it means. Moreover, to lend credibility to his testimony and avoid having it discredited on cross-examination he must profess absolute certainty about what he saw or heard. This leaves the veracity of trial testimony always open to question.[389]

Ponder this again. "Do the Rules take their bearings by what most lawyers should do or by what they in fact do?"[390] "In a nutshell, lawyers need to admit to themselves, their clients, and the general public that the benefits of litigation are overrated, with lawyers sometimes being the only real 'winners.'"[391]

DISCOVERY

> Discovery is the process by which one side can request information from the other side. Under rules of discovery, one party can request to interview another side's witnesses, require the other side to produce documents from its files, or answer extensive written questions about its behavior with which the lawsuit is concerned.[392]

The *ABA Model Rules of Professional Conduct* is rather sparse as to discovery requirements. Rule 3.4, entitled *Fairness to Opposing Party and Counsel*, merely says that "a lawyer shall not...(d) in pretrial procedure, make a frivolous discovery request or fail to make reasonably diligent effort to comply with a legally proper discovery request by an opposing party."[393] The Rule contains a comment that says, "the procedure of the adversary system contemplates that the evidence in a case is to be marshalled competitively by the con-

---

388. Journal, December 1992, p. 112
389. Journal, January 1991, p. 60
390. Journal, September 1990, p. 71
391. Horn, p. 15
392. Neely, p. 183
393. Rules, p. 80

tending parties."[394] In other words, every man for himself, which is consistent with the adversarial system.

Lawyer Katz had several things to say about discovery.

> Discovery has taken on a life of its own as a way of *preventing and bypassing* the courtroom, and as a weapon of intimidation and outright extortion. Under these circumstances, the most ruthless side has the advantage.[395]

> During the pre-trial period, the months or years between the date the plaintiff files the lawsuit and the start of the courtroom trial, rules regarding discovery are the most important. These govern how the parties develop the facts by use of different tools and techniques, including interrogatories (written requests for answers), depositions (sworn statements), and the production of "documents and things." Each of these areas has its own set of sub-rules.

> The rules governing discovery mandate an extremely broad right to seek information—a right established in its present form only a half century ago... [quoting a Federal Rule of Procedure] parties may obtain discovery regarding any matter, not privileged, which is relevant to the subject matter involved in the pending action.[396]

> Running up the opponent's tab is not hard. Discovery essentially involves three procedures: interrogatories, depositions, and document subpoenas. Each is vulnerable to deliberate and extensive abuse.... Interrogatories are written questionnaires that demand written responses from the other side...not necessarily admissible in court as evidence. Depositions involve asking questions in person. A party can demand that adverse party or non-party witnesses appear to be questioned under oath. Neither judge nor jury is present for deposition questioning....Document subpoenas are used to demand written materials."[397]

Judge Rothwax was not a fan of discovery, at least in criminal cases.

> We also have discovery rules. These were originally intended to aid in the search for truth, but it doesn't really work that way because discovery is not entirely reciprocal. The discovery statutes require the prosecution to turn over all of its files and information to the defendant's attorney, but in most jurisdictions the defendant's attorney

---

394. Rules, p. 80
395. Katz, pp. 70,71
396. Katz, p. 25
397. Katz, p. 69

does not have the same obligation.... Once the defendant knows what the prosecution's evidence is, he may build his case around refuting it. In this way, discovery may impede the truth, not further it.[398]

Judge Rothwax explained it more fully. "Even in states where reciprocal discovery is required, the balance is not equalized. Since the Fifth Amendment protects defendants from compulsory self-incrimination, as a practical matter, reciprocal discovery does not meaningfully exist."[399] Yet, "defense attorneys argue that discovery from the defense is unfair, even if constitutional, because it eases the DA's burden of proving guilt."[400] If the accused is in fact guilty, then the prosecutor should not be made to suffer a difficult time in proving it. If the accused is in fact innocent, then no valid reason exists for the defense attorney to harass the prosecution and be fearful of discovery.

Discovery was originally initiated in the belief that it would help to counteract the problems created by the adversarial process and, in doing so, reduce the costs. It hasn't worked that way. In 1982, Judge Neely wrote that during his ten years as a judge "discovery has gotten more exhaustive"[401] Judge Rothwax described a case that "centered around the belief that discovery led not to greater fact finding and pursuit of truth but to just the opposite—a tendency to perjury and falsification."[402]

Professor McElhaney said that "the point of discovery is not to get into a fight, it's to get ready for trial."[403] Since, in civil cases, suits are often filed as mere fishing expeditions,[404] discovery or some form of disclosure may be desirable, although McElhaney has stated that "discovery is not the best way to learn the basic facts of a case. In fact, it is probably the most expensive and inefficient way to gather information."[405]

---

398. Rothwax, p. 28
399. Rothwax, p. 179
400. Rothwax, p. 180
401. Neely, p. 185
402. Rothwax, p. 176
403. Journal, February 1999, p. 72
404. Rembar, p. 250. See also, Journal, December 1991, p. 80
405. Journal, December 1989, p. 76

RESTRICTIONS ON EVIDENCE

"The term 'procedure' relates to the machinery of justice, to the form, manner, and order of conducting suits and prosecutions."[406] All that occurs in the courtroom during a trial is based upon what is deemed proper procedure, a system developed over a long period of time by reason of the Constitution, court interpretations of the Constitution, customs, laws, rules, and precedent. However, "the Constitution is what the judges say it is."[407] "Courts are stickier...about small errors in cases where life or liberty is at stake. It would be no surprise, then, to find that the law of criminal procedure outdid civil procedure in record worship and technical artifice."[408]

"A legal system must make provisions for conducting orderly trials and hearings; it must contain rules of evidence that guarantee rational procedures of inquiry. While there are variations in these procedures, the rule of law requires some form of due process: that is, a process reasonably designed to ascertain the truth"[409] While considering the rules of evidence, one should contemplate whether they do, in fact, facilitate ascertaining the truth. In doing so, also think how the rules of evidence might well be different in the absence of adversaryism.

"The rules of evidence...focus on exclusion."[410] Exclusion has to do with those matters that cannot be introduced at a trial, therefore are excluded. These matters may actually be relevant facts, but for one reason or another, they are prohibited, that is, excluded, from being presented at trial. Exclusion is used by the courts to control deemed unlawful acts committed, primarily by law enforcement, prior to trial. Apparently, the courts believe, erroneously actually, that by doing so they will stop the alleged misconduct. In these instances, the courts are more focused on technicalities, the alleged misbehavior, than they are in the inno-

---

406. Post, p. 105
407. Post, p. 7
408. Friedman(2), p. 150
409. Rawls, p. 239
410. Rembar, p. 326

cence or guilt of those who are accused. Here is how Judge Neely explains it.

> The average citizen confronted by daily street crime asks, 'Why?' Every time some felon's constitutional rights are vindicated, he is back on the street committing more crimes. It would appear at first blush that the Supreme Court has a screw loose. Certainly, the object of the whole exercise was not to release the guilty or to protect the criminal class at the expense of everyone else. Rather, the object was to effect a change in the way all the enforcement institutions of government operated. But the only tool available to the federal courts, however, was their power to require evidence to be excluded. Another instance, if you will, of trying to do brain surgery with a meat ax.[411]

Most exclusionary rules have to do with the Fourth (unreasonable searches and seizures), the Fifth (shall not be compelled to be a witness against himself), or the Sixth (right to assistance of counsel) Amendments, although in New York there are "between twenty and thirty exclusionary rules under which evidence might be suppressed."[412] As Judge Rothwax explained, the issues concerning the exclusionary rules "often have nothing to do with whether the defendant is innocent or guilty."[413]

Judge Neely stated that the procedural rules leading to excluded evidence are difficult even for lawyers to master.[414] Judge Rothwax confirmed that this is true of police as well. "The legal doctrines the exclusionary rule enforces are so complicated and tangled that the police (and even judges themselves) cannot determine in advance what a majority of the Supreme Court will find. If the police do not understand the rules, how can they enforce them?"[415]

Judge Rothwax then continued. "Say what you will about justice, the hallmarks of the exclusionary rule are irrationality, arbitrariness, and a lack of proportion, Whenever it is applied, a criminal goes free—no matter how serious the crime or minor the

---

411. Neely, p. 137
412. Rothwax, p. 26
413. Rothwax, p. 27
414. Neely, p. 142
415. Rothwax, p. 64

police intrusion."[416] Long ago, British reformer Jeremy Bentham said that "exclusionary rules...had the perverse effect of shutting the door against the truth: the rules gave 'license to oppression by all imaginable wrongs.'"[417] It seems that no one is keen about the exclusionary rules except the US Supreme Court and, of course, the criminal defense attorneys, not a good mix.

Judge Rothwax made an obvious observation. "If you suppress evidence, you're suppressing truth.... Remember, there is never any question of the reliability of the evidence.... Rejection of evidence does nothing to punish the wrong-doing official, while it may, and likely will, release the wrong-doing defendant."[418]

An editorial in the Cedar Rapids Gazette had this to say about exclusionary rules. "Is tossing all this evidence out of court really in the best interest of criminal justice?...Why can't a judge weigh the value of the evidence against the harm suffered by the defendant?...not all evidence-gathering errors grievously impinge on the defendant's rights. Too much evidence is being automatically tossed out of court. Too many criminals are walking. There is a big need for a little common sense regarding the rules of legal evidence."[419]

Whereas the exclusionary rules are adopted children of the courts, the due process of law clauses in the Constitution were conceived by the Fifth Amendment (ratified December 15, 1791), which pertains to the federal government, and the Fourteenth Amendment (ratified July 9, 1868), which pertains to the states. These provisions provide that no person shall "be deprived of life, liberty, or property, without due process of law." According to Judge Fleming,

> the original meaning of due process comprehended law in its regular course of administration through courts of justice, and the due process clause originally operated merely to place certain procedures beyond the reach of the legislative process. In the words of Story,

---

416. Rothwax, p. 64
417. Friedman(2), p. 154
418. Rothwax, pp. 62,63
419. Gazette, August 22, 1989, p.4A

"This clause in effect affirms the right of trial according to the process and proceedings of the common law."[420]

Due process of law "was built upon the simple idea that a trial should be a live contest over disputed facts between a defendant and his accusers."[421] It is doubtful that the protection of life, liberty, and the pursuit of happiness hinges upon adversaryism.

One of the restrictions on evidence is the hearsay rule. According to Rembar, "in a broad statement it is simple: a witness shall speak only of his own perceptions, not of someone else's, and a document is evidence only of itself, not of things outside itself.... He may speak only of what he knows directly, not of what another person told him.... The reasons for the hearsay rule are plain enough.... Secondhand information...is often unreliable."[422]

Professor McElhaney prefers to call the hearsay rule the real witness rule. "The purpose of the rule is to preserve the rights of confrontation and cross-examination because they are essential to the evaluation of the witness by the judge and jury.... When the real witness is not on the stand, we are left with hearsay.... When you ask who you want to cross-examine, the answer depends on whether the truth of the out-of-court statement matters. If the truth of the out-of-court statement doesn't make any difference, the real witness is on the stand and the statement isn't hearsay."[423]

Judge Neely labels the hearsay rule an "artificial" rule of evidence. Continuing, he says that "there are so many exceptions to the hearsay rule that the exceptions almost obliterate the rule. As a result, for every rule of evidence excluding testimony there is a countervailing exception to the rule that lets the testimony in."[424]

Professor Maechling says that the hearsay rule distorts the judicial process. "In the adversarial process the jury is not allowed to hear what the witness says another person told him he heard or saw at the time.... This wipes out a whole area of valuable information

---

420. Fleming, p. 90
421. Knight, p. 69
422. Rembar, pp. 330,332
423. Journal, March 2003, p. 53
424. Neely, p. 99

that is especially useful in the prosecution of conspiracies, racke-teering and white-collar crimes."[425]

While some exceptions with the hearsay rule still exist, the US Supreme Court has recently made an exception more difficult by holding in Crawford v. Washington that "the Sixth Amendment's confrontation clause [which requires the accused 'to be confronted with the witnesses against him'] requires that defendants be allowed to examine testimony against them."[426] In the Crawford case, Justice Antonin Scalia wrote that "where testimonial evidence is at issue, the Sixth Amendment demands what the common law required: unavailability and a prior opportunity for cross-exami-nation."[427] The word "testimonial" is going to be an issue, but think how this decision will affect child and spouse abuse cases as well as cases involving incompetents and perhaps even rape. Try to envision a two-year old being cross-examined. Pity the prosecutor or plaintiff's attorney.

Former prosecutor Bugliosi wrote, after the Simpson trial but prior to the Crawford case, that "although a defendant in a criminal trial has the absolute right—under the Confrontation Clause of the Sixth Amendment to the United States Constitution—to cross-examine witnesses against him, the nature and extent of that cross-examination is not absolute."[428] That sounds a bit like double talk, but perhaps that is because the hearsay rule is involved.

WITNESSES

"The law of evidence...is a matter of who may speak and what they may say.... It is usually stated in negative form—exclusionary rules, generalizations of what the courts will not listen to."[429] Due to the "adversary nature of the proceeding...witnesses are called on

425. Journal, January 1991, p. 60
426. Journal, September 2004, p. 22
427. Journal, September 2004, p. 22
428. Bugliosi, p.67
429. Rembar, p. 325

behalf of the parties rather than on behalf of the court."[430] That does not mean, however, that the called witness will, or is allowed to, testify. The opposing attorney may object either as to the right of the witness to testify or as to what the witness says or is asked to say. As to testimony or proffered testimony, it may be challenged as being irrelevant, incompetent, or immaterial, or some form thereof, technical objections that vex even experienced trial attorneys. These restrictions on testimony are believed to be the result of the distrust of the jurors.[431] So it is said that it is up to the lawyers and judges to keep out testimony that the jurors might not give proper credence to.

"On the stand, the witness is to relate his observations of an event. He must tell what he saw or heard, and even touched or smelled or tasted. He cannot, however, offer a subjective opinion unless he is an expert witness."[432] Testimony that comes in, however, need not just sit there as the gospel truth. One of the things that the opposing attorney may do under the adversarial procedure is to cross-examine the witness. Listen to this explanation.

> The purpose of cross-examination is to weaken the testimony the witness has given, or, at best, negate it, or, less spectacular but highly useful, to do no more than clarify ambiguous responses. The cross-examiner seeks to show inadequacy of observation, confusion, bias, inconsistency, even contradiction.... The fight is fine; it suits the adversary system.[433]

It is often said that cross-examination is "the greatest engine ever invented for the discovery of truth."[434] That statement has about the same ring of truth as the statement that trumpets the US judicial system as being the best in the world. Professor Maechling says this about cross-examination.

> The adversarial system is at its worst in the ritual of cross-examination. The witness who tries to give a frank and honest statement of

---

430. Farnsworth, p. 114
431. Rembar, p. 321
432. Post, p. 131
433. Rembar, p. 337
434. Journal, July 1992, p. 78

his observations, impressions and beliefs, with all the necessary qualifications, will find his recollection challenged at every step. In most cases he will be forced to retract or to restate only those portions that he can testify to with precision and absolute certainty. Ostensibly designed to narrow testimony down to a hard core of 'fact,' cross-examination more often confuses the witness and muddies the record. This is exactly what the cross-examiner intends...the accusatorial process, which emphasizes the extortion of 'yes' or 'no' answers, can easily turn cross-examination under oath into a game of entrapment.[435]

As most everyone knows, a witness is not allowed to volunteer information nor to explain or elaborate on his or her answers, nor, especially, to argue with the questioner. A witness is on the stand merely to answer questions, some of which are to confuse, not to elicit information. "witnesses are interrogated one at a time and do not confront each other"[436] As a result, not only is the witness thoroughly frustrated, so is truth.

Lillian S. Fisher, Judge of the Pima County Superior Court in Tucson, Arizona, once said that "I know that a witness may testify truthfully, but that he is precluded from telling the whole truth. Because of the rules of evidence, I know, and the attorneys involved know, that if a witness did 'tell the truth, the whole truth and nothing but the truth,' there would be a mistrial, a new trial or a motion to dismiss."[437] In addition, Professor Langbein said that "so much of what passes for cross-examination in our procedure is deliberately truth-defeating."[438] Note the word "deliberately." In other words, intentionally. Not always, of course, as exceptions always exist.

In criminal cases, what about the defendant who refuses to testify? "The defendant is competent to take the witness stand and testify, as might any other witness, in his own behalf, but he cannot be compelled to do so and failure to testify creates no presumption

---

435. Journal, January 1991, pp. 60,62
436. Farnsworth, p. 112
437. Journal, September 29, 1986, p. 8
438. Landsman, p. 65

against him and generally may not be commented upon by the pros-ecution."[439] Lawyer Knight has a comment about this.

> The privilege against self-incrimination fits into the logic of our justice system with precision. It is a corollary of the presumption of innocence, and of the state's burden of proving guilt beyond a reason-able doubt. If there is such a presumption and such a burden, it fol-lows that an accused can sit in pristine silence and dare the state to do its worst with the evidence it has. If that very silence can be treated as evidence of guilt, how can it be said that innocence is pre-sumed?[440]

Former prosecutor Bugliosi had this to say about this topic.

> No sound in any courtroom is as loud as the defendant's silence when he is accused of the most serous crime of all, murder, and he chooses not to deny it from the witness stand. When a person is falsely accused of a murder, it should take a team of wild horses to keep him from the witness stand.[441]

Judge Rothwax felt that the privilege against self-incrimi-nation "is an unfair limitation on the pursuit of justice."[442] In spite of what Knight seemed to have said, he agreed with the judge when he wrote that "The idea that one could say nothing in response to a creditable accusation and not have his silence considered against him is neither obvious nor, many have argued, particularly logical. Some dedicated critics have even said that it is bizarre."[443] All Knight had said previously was that the privilege fits into our justice system. In other words, perhaps our justice system is a bit bizarre, too. Contrary to the US system , in civil law jurisdictions the accused "can refuse to answer questions. However, a negative inference may be drawn from his refusal to answer and anything he does say may be used against him."[444]

Expert testimony has its own problems. Here is what Pro-fessor Langbein has to say about so-called experts.

---

439. Farnsworth, p. 112
440. Knight, p. 98. See also, Rembar, p. 397
441. Bugliosi, p. 25
442. Rothwax, p. 29
443. Knight, p. 90
444. Journal, January 1991, p. 62

At the American trial bar, those of us who serve as expert witnesses are known as "saxophones".... The idea is that the lawyer plays
the tune, manipulating the expert as though the expert were a musi-
cal instrument on which the lawyer sounds the desired notes.... I have
experienced the subtle pressures to join the team—to shade one's
views, to conceal doubt, to overstate nuance, to downplay weak
aspects of the case that one has been hired to bolster. Nobody likes to
disappoint a patron; and beyond this psychological pressure is the
financial inducement.... The more measured and impartial an expert
is, the less likely he is to be used by either side.[445]

Although expert testimony has its own problems, a far greater
problem has to do with the testimony of the ordinary, average
witness, including the testimony of the parties themselves. As you
read the following quote, consider that much of what is said would
not and could not occur if adversaryism were not our chosen system
of justice. Trial lawyers try to convince us that truth results from
adversarial processes. A good cross-examination, they say, will
result in the truth being found. That is not true since winning is the
goal, not finding the truth. Now read what writer Mark Curriden,
who covers legal topics for the Chattanooga, Tennessee, *Times*, has
to say.

[There is] a surprising and quite disturbing truth about the US
legal system: People can come into court, place their left hand on a
Bible, raise their right hand heavenward and state the traditional
oath...only to proceed to lie through their teeth. And they will probably get away with it...[quoting Marvin H. Shoob, Senior US District
Court Judge in Atlanta] "No one is talking about it. No one is admitting we have a serious problem on our hands. Perjury is like a naughty
word never to be admitted or discussed publicly. It's the justice system's dirty little secret that no one wants to admit or confront."....
Perhaps a growing prevalence of perjury should not be surprising in a
legal system that emphasizes adversarial advocacy...[then, quoting
Professor Hazard, as director of the American Law Institute in Philadelphia, an expert on legal ethics] "Yes, shading the truth and telling
lies occurs in almost every case.... But we have created this adversarial
system that encourages it."[446]

---

445. Landsman, p. 61
446. Journal, May 1995, pp. 68,69

PLEA-BARGAINING—THE ILLUSION OF JUSTICE

Plea-bargaining is a device whereby criminal defendants admit, in other words plead guilty, to a lesser offence or to a portion of the total charges against them in order to avoid being found guilty of a greater offense or greater number of offenses. Although Judge Neely did not have plea-bargaining in mind, what he said could apply. "Far more perfect justice is achieved by designing rules that expedite settlements and encourage people to sort out their own problems on some reasonable basis."[447] Judge Rothwax claimed that "no one likes the necessity of plea-bargaining. It is a simple fact that plea-bargaining sacrifices those values the unworkable system of adversary jury trial is meant to serve"[448] Lawyer Kagan describes plea bargaining as "coercive" and "tawdry"—"the ugly but affordable offspring of the woefully costly and inefficient American jury trial."[449]

For the overall good of the judicial system, for instance by uncluttering the docket, it would seem that plea-bargaining has some merits. But the US Supreme court, with its usual wisdom, has placed quite a burden on the trial judge, as Judge Fleming explains.

> The trial judge is now required to interrogate at length a defendant who wishes to enter a guilty plea, even though defendant is represented by counsel present in court. The interrogation must show that the plea is intelligent and voluntary, that defendant has waived his privilege against self-incrimination, that defendant has waived his right to a jury trial, that defendant has waived his right to confront his accusers, and that defendant possesses a full understanding of the connotations and consequences of his plea.[450]

Judge Rothwax pointed out that not everyone is entitled to plea-bargaining, due principally to the seriousness of the crime.[451] "In order for plea bargaining to be meaningful, there has to be a rela-

---

447. Neely, pp. 122,123
448. Rothwax, p. 150
449. Kagan, p. 89
450. Fleming, p. 85
451. Rothwax, p. 162

tionship between the seriousness of the charge, the strength of the charge, and the sentence that is imposed."[452]

Although speaking in another context, Judge Posner perhaps discloses a reason why plea-bargaining is so prevalent.

> Rather than equalize the resources of prosecutors and defendants, the legal system has erected formidable procedural obstacles to conviction. These have succeeded in reducing the probability of convicting innocent persons to an extremely low level, but the price is that many guilty persons are acquitted...or are never charged, or are allowed to plead guilty to crimes much less serious than those they actually committed.[453]

Professor Maechling believes that plea-bargaining has some benefits "as long as it is limited to one individual; it has the practical benefit of saving the state from the expense and effort of time-consuming trials and appeals, and from overloading the system. But once transformed into an instrument for convicting conspirators and co-defendants, it opens the door to dishonesty and gross injustice."[454]

No true observer believes that the plea bargaining process is always fair to the accused. One of these is public defender Howard Finkelstein, head of the public defender's office in Florida's Broward County. Upon being elected head of the office, he put an end to what is labeled "meet-and-greet pleas." In doing so, Finkelstein stated that he was worried "that the practice ran afoul of the Sixth Amendment's right to effective assistance of counsel as well as ethics standards set out in the ABA Model Rules of Professional Conduct...They're making this life-altering decision in a matter of several minutes while handcuffed in the middle of a courtroom surrounded by all of these people...That's not fair. That's not just. That's not equal. Defendants with the financial means to hire private lawyers do not face the same plight. If you look very carefully, what you see are two different systems of justice, two different standards and two different approaches."[455]

---

452. Rothwax, p. 164
453. Posner, p. 207
454. Journal, January 1991, p. 60

Before issuing his new policy, Finkelstein consulted with Randolph Braccialarghe, a law professor at Nova Southeastern University in Fort Lauderdale, Fla., and a former Broward County prosecutor. Braccialarghe agreed, saying "meet-and-greet pleas fail to meet ethics standards,"[456] William O. Whitehurst, Austin, Texas, attorney who chairs the ABA Standing Committee on Legal Aid and Indigent Defendants, also agreed, he stating "this is wonderful. It takes people who will stand up like this lawyer has done and say, 'Hey, look, we've got a problem with this system.'"[457] And so did Malia Brink, indigent defense counsel for the National Association of Criminal Defense Lawyers, who noted "that the standards require a lawyer to independently investigate the case against his or her client...[the policy change is] incredibly admirable and absolutely correct...I think meet-and-greet pleas are a problematic practice that exists, unfortunately, throughout the country."[458]

455. www.abanet.org/journal/ereport/jn24plead.html, June 24, 2005, p. 1
456. www.abanet.org/journal/ereport/jn24plead.html, June 24, 2005, p. 1
457. www.abanet.org/journal/ereport/jn24plead.html, June 24, 2005, p. 2
458. www.abanet.org/journal/ereport/jn24plead.html, June 24, 2005, p. 2

CHAPTER 6. THE JUDGES

THE ROLE OF THE JUDGES

Prosecutor Bugliosi has a rather lengthy observation about the reputation of judges.

> A word about judges. The American people have an understandably negative view of politicians, public opinion polls show, and an equally negative view of lawyers. David Kennedy, professor of history at Stanford University, in writing about politicians, says: "With the possible exception of lawyers, we hold no other professionals in such contempt. Who among us can utter the word "politician" without a sneer?' Conventional logic would seem to dictate, then, that since a judge is normally both a politician and a lawyer, people would have an opinion of them lower than a grasshopper's belly. But on the contrary, a $25 black cotton robe elevates the denigrated lawyer-politician to a position of considerable honor and respect in our society, as if the garment itself miraculously imbued the person with qualities not previously possessed...This depiction ignores reality.[459]

In saying that, Bugliosi was rather contemptuous of those jurisdictions, state as well as federal, that make political judicial appointments. In this respect, the American Judicature Society "has completed its Judicial Selection in the States Web site

---

459. Bugliosi, p. 87

[www.ajs.org/js]. It provides detailed information of all aspects of the judicial selection process in each of the 50 states and the District of Columbia."[460]

Regardless, an ABA Journal article states that there has been a "considerable change in the role of judges over the past decade or so. Among those changes are the increased number of litigants representing themselves—who sometimes need the court's help in procedural matters—and judges in specialty courts who step out of the role of umpire and get involved in matters."[461]

In the view of Judge Posner, "Judges make rather than find law."[462] This is also the view of lawyer Spence. "The judges of America have more influence over the course of the nation than Congress and the president. They interpret the laws, apply them, change them to match their private vision of the world, and extend their collective nose into every manner of private or government business...They make law...They are omnipotent."[463] Now we again get to this heady stuff, like "the best damn system in the world." Former ABA President N. Lee Cooper of Birmingham, Alabama, says that "we have the finest judiciary on earth."[464]

In describing the trial judge, Judge Frankel takes a more realistic view.

> The judge is in familiar theory the impartial director of the trial as well as the decision-maker. The judicial umpire regulates the contest, then decides who won. The office carries in theory large powers of direction in the courtroom, mitigated and justified by entire neutrality. The practice reflects the theory, but incompletely. In fact, the judge's managerial powers are limited by procedures that give to the lawyers, not to the judge, the functions of initiating, organizing, and conducting the courtroom struggle...With exceptions, as always, our trial judges tend to be recruited from the ranks of people with substantial experience as trial lawyers...Trial lawyers are the gladiators...It is also plausible to wonder whether years of partisan combat are necessarily ideal training for the qualities of detachment and calm

460. Lawyer, June 2004, p. 27
461. Journal, April 2004, p. 67
462. Journal, September 1990, p. 100
463. Spence, p. 92
464. Journal, August 1997, p. 8

reflection that we suppose ourselves to desire on the bench. [The courtroom tactics of the trial attorneys] leads the judge toward qualities and responses that are, in one word, adversarial.[465]

When a trial is before a jury, some overlapping exists between the duties of the judge and the jury. Professor Farnsworth describes it this way. "It is the task of the jury, at least in theory, to decide issues of 'fact,' and that of the judge to decide issues of 'law.' The dividing line between the two is often a shadowy one, and, for example, whether the jury's decision on an issue of 'fact' has been reasonable is itself an issue of 'law.'"[466] No doubt exists, though, that it is the judges who "enforce rules of evidence."[467]

But, says writer Post "however certain the rules may be, 'the decisions remain at the mercy of the courts' fact-finding.'"[468] That may be true at the trial court level, but at the appellate level, it is not the facts that are so terribly important, it is how the facts were determined, in other words the legal procedure used at trial or even prior thereto. Professor Landsman says that "reliance on elaborate sets of rules to structure the adversary process also helps to promote the use of appellate courts. These courts see to it that litigants and judges comply with mandated rules and procedures."[469] Professor Landsman then explains the development and significance of the adversarial process.

> These [appellate] courts were committed to a careful search of the record to determine if there was error warranting reversal. The emphasis on the search for error may have been what led nineteenth century courts to a preoccupation with technical nicety...the development of adversarial principles may have had much to do with it...Whatever the cause of strict review, it did help to establish the adversarial principle that trial activity would have to conform to the rules vesting the litigants with control of the process and securing the neutrality and passivity of the fact finder.[470]

---

465. Landsman, pp. 87-89
466. Farnsworth, p. 103
467. Olson, p. 110
468. Post, p. 131
469. Landsman, p. 5
470. Landsman, p. 19

Lawyer Spence makes the observation that "no one really supervises judges."[471] On the other hand, Judge Posner points out that "the position of the [trial] judge, as a person called on to resolve a dispute in a manner almost certain to harm one party and benefit the other, is inherently precarious."[472] Judge Neely describes trial judges thusly.

> Judges are not machines. They are living, breathing, emotional, political, passionate human beings with definite ideas about the equity of any given lawsuit...judges work backward from their intuitive grasp of the equities of a lawsuit to a manipulation of legal rules that will achieve what they consider an equitable result. Different trial judges will handle the same lawsuit in entirely different ways, producing contrary results.[473]

"Thus," as writer Post notes, "the judicial system itself can retard or further the realization of justice...The judicial system itself...can be a major aid or hindrance to justice. Even more crucial, however, for justice, are the judges: no matter how excellent a court system may be on paper, no matter how good it may be philosophically, it will never be any better than the men who administer it."[474]

Lawyer Kagan wrote that in "German and French courts, where bureaucratically recruited and embedded judges—not the parties' lawyers and not lay juries—dominate both the evidence-gathering and the decisionmaking processes."[475] Later, he stated that "American lawyers do more because American judges do less."[476] Most American trial lawyers would not want it otherwise.

---

471. Spence, p. 266
472. Posner, p.6
473. Neely, p. 109
474. Post, p. 13
475. Kagan, p. 11
476. Kagan, p. 105

JUDICIAL NEGLECT

Actually, according to lawyers Katz and Crier, judges could do much more.

> Judges can become more proactive in dealing with the game-playing. Judges...have the means to curb many of the egregious abuses. They can assert their authority to manage the cases on their dockets so that substance again becomes more important than process. Judges can also accomplish much through revisions of court rules and procedures.[477]

> Judges should be as liberal with their sanctions against unethical or obstreperous lawyers as those attorneys are with the damage figures they request in their pleadings. Assertions in bad faith, discovery abuses, and tactics to delay and harass should all result in monetary sanctions against the attorneys or even dismissal of the case itself in the most flagrant situations. Judges should be willing to grant motions for summary judgment to dispose of frivolous claims as soon as possible in the litigation process.[478]

Lawyer Rembar pointed out that present day legal procedures are not much different today than they were years ago: "Why is it odd to clear away legal questions first, decide which facts are relevant, and then proceed to proof?...Trial judges...still do their most significant work before the trial begins...Most major rulings...are made in advance of trial...For the most part, judgment precedes proof...There is nothing odd about it."[479]

Some feel that judges "are merely referees in the courtroom, making sure the adversaries stay within the rules of evidence." While others feel that "judges are seekers of truth and justice, not just referees...judges should make comments...should tell witnesses when they are being less than truthful."[480] Former Federal District Court Judge Hubert Will would agree with the latter. "The responsibility of the judge is to be superintendent of the production of justice—the traditional concept of judge as a skilled referee is

---

477. Katz, pp. 14,145
478. Crier, p. 211
479. Rembar, p. 232
480. Journal, May 1995, p. 72

incompatible with production of highest quality of justice."[481] And so would Judge Rothwax. "It is the judge, ultimately, who must control the courtroom, rein in the lawyers, and instill a sense of dignity and sobriety to the process. I truly believe that judges get the lawyers they deserve."[482]

Trial judges are not the only judges that should use a bit of common sense. An editorial in the Cedar Rapids Gazette[483] took to task an Iowa Supreme Court decision[484] that held that a man was still obligated to pay child support even though it was later proven through genetic testing that he was not the father of the child. The editorial stated the obvious. "Public respect for the law surely cannot be elevated by...providing yet another example that the search for truth and justice takes distant second priority to the search for technicalities."[485]

In states where judges are chosen and retained through the political process [note: according to Crier, "Texas is one of eight states that hold partisan elections for their high courts...a total of thirty-nine states elect some of their judiciary."[486]], judges tread cautiously, but almost all trial judges are "fearful of intervening, often uninformed about the details of the case, and unable to comment on the evidence."[487] Judge Rothwax adds that "committed to the search for truth, the judge is also required by the rules of the game to sit by helplessly while skilled professionals are engaged in clear, deliberate, and entirely 'proper' efforts to frustrate the search."[488] Professor Landsman attempts to explain how all this is consistent with the US system of justice.

> The adversary system relies on a neutral and passive decision maker to adjudicate disputes after they have been aired by the adver-

---

481. Landsman, p. 94

482. Rothwax, pp. 135,136

483. Gazette, June 3, 1995, p. 6A

484. State Ex Rel Baumgartner v. Wilcox, 532 N. W. 2d 774 (Iowa 1995)

485. Gazette, June 3, 1995, p. 6A

486. Crier, p. 191

487. Rothwax, p. 29

488. Rothwax, p. 227

saries in a contested proceeding. The decision-maker is expected to refrain from making any judgments until the conclusion of the contest and is prohibited from becoming actively involved in the gathering of evidence or the settlement of the case. Adversary theory suggest that if the decision-maker strays from the passive role, she runs a serious risk of prematurely committing herself to one or another version of the facts and of failing to appreciate the value of all the evidence...Where judges are assigned a neutral and passive function...they will, in all likelihood, be expected to devote their energies to resolving the disputes framed by the litigants. One of the most significant implications of the American adoption of the principles of neutrality and passivity is that it tends to commit the adversary system to the objective of resolving disputes rather than searching for material truth.[489]

Sometimes judges are helpless, but sometimes they are cautious. According to Newman Flannigan, Executive Director of the National District Attorneys Association, Alexandria, Virginia, "Judges are afraid of being reversed, so they let anything by the defendant in."[490] But that isn't the complete answer to the problem. Lawyer Kagan explains why.

Underlying [the judge's] passivity, I suspect, is a set of beliefs shaped by adversarial legalism: the lawyers for both sides, not the judges, are responsible for bringing out the relevant evidence. It also is risky for a judge to depart from the adversarial script, for an appellate court might find that he has transgressed the defendant's constitutional rights. Finally, in the system's list of goals, following the adversarial procedures properly ranks somewhat higher than determining the truth.[491]

Still, the weaknesses of the adversarial process are slowly being recognized, albeit unconsciously. Professor Landsman believes that "in recent years, judges have been freed to take an active part in both the preparation and presentation of lawsuits...Rules regulating judicial involvement in the trial have been steadily liberalized...These changes have appreciably altered the adversary process by encouraging judicial management at the expense of party control of proceedings. As judicial power has

---

489. Landsman, pp. 2,3
490. Journal, October 1995, p. 58
491. Kagan, p. 244

increased, the primacy of the jury in adversary proceedings has been reduced."[492]

Professor Saltzburg recognized that "the trend seems to be to let the judge become more active, to let the judge search for truth, to let the judge do what he believes must be done in order to provide a 'fair trial' for the litigants." But that thought seems to terrify him because he continues "but...the trial judge who attempts to usurp control from the parties compromises the integrity of the bench and often threatens the independence of the jury...it is dangerous for the trial judge to explore new territory with any witness"[493]

In part, at least, Tampa lawyer, C. Steven Yerrid, who has great confidence in his own abilities, would agree.

> In the arena of the courtroom, a lawsuit should never be unfairly determined by the 'robes,' as trial lawyers often call presiding judges in reference to the black robes they wear in court. The advocates should neither be aided nor hindered in any significant way by the judge. Assuming the rules are not violated, the parties being represented should be the combatants and the lawyers should be the champions of the cause, with the outcome resolved only by the advocacy that prevails.[494]

Yet journalist Curriden insists that "lawyers on both sides of the bar maintain that judges are not doing enough to police the 'backdooring' of evidence or raising of tangential issues."[495] Keep in mind, though, that judges sit on a small island surrounded by sharks. According to Judge Rothwax "a trial is a minefield, and any judicial misstep—or even a perceived misstep—can lead to a reversal of the verdict, with no consideration of whether the defendant is guilty or not."[496]

According to Elliot Bien's *Viewpoint* in *Judicature*,[497] bar associations are an ineffective means to correct deficiencies in our judicial system, that it will be up to the judiciary to do so.

---

492. Landsman, p. 23
493. Landsman, p. 121
494. Yerrid, p. 194
495. Journal, October 1995, p. 58
496. Rothwax, p. 31
497. Judicature, November-December 2002, p. 132

JUDICIAL ACTIVISM

Judges have always had the authority to control misbehavior of trial attorneys.[498] Judges expect civility and courtesy and will generally react to a lack of common decency. Judges have a right to keep tight control of the courtroom and in that sense, such control may be considered judicial activism, but it is not the kind of activism envisioned by flag-waving out in the streets.

More likely, it is considered judicial activism when a court, particularly an appellate court, in effect legislates, that is, creates new law that actually should be the prerogative of a legislature. None of that is what is contemplated here, however. Judicial activism, in the sense used here, has to do with the trial judge "butting in" the case itself, such as taking over some of the trial proceedings, interfering with a trial lawyer's presentation of the evidence, or summing up the evidence to a jury. It is assumed that these particular judicial activities occur when a judge becomes disenchanted with the adversary process.

> According to one line of thinking, judges are merely referees in the courtroom, making sure the adversaries stay within the rules of evidence. Others, however, believe judges should become more active in policing testimony. 'Judges are seekers of truth and justice, not just referees,' according to...(Professor) Hazard...who maintains that 'judges should make comments. They should tell witnesses when they are being less than truthful.'"[499]

Lawyer Katz seems to agree when she writes about judges taking "back the courtroom" and especially reining, "in attorneys whose tactics become too aggressive or abrasive, or clearly questionable...In addition to enforcing standards of decorum and conduct, judges are being advised to draw upon an array of management techniques."[500] However, she sounds dispirited when she adds that "it is also becoming clear that modest and conventional

---

498. Journal, July 1997, p. 97
499. Journal, May 1995
500. Katz, p. 101

reform packages and improved managerial techniques are not sufficient to redeem the system.[501]

Professor Landsman had this to say while discussing the limits of neutrality and passivity of the trial judge.

> It is a fundamental principle of the adversary system that the decision maker remain passive while the parties develop facts upon which a decision may be based. If the fact finder strays too far from passivity adversary theory suggests that neutrality will be jeopardized...It is asserted by many within the judicial establishment that the passive judge wastes time, is vulnerable to manipulation by counsel and is likely to be distracted from uncovering the 'truth.'...At the heart of the debate about managerial judging remains the question whether activist judges can fulfill the expectations created by America's reliance on adversarial procedure.[502]

Professor Landsman admits that the adversarial system is criticized because "it places the trial judge in the untenable position of having to perform inconsistent or conflicting tasks,"[503] a situation Judge Frankel describes this way. "Because the judge is obliged to control the litigation and the litigants, it is extremely difficult for her to remain neutral and passive."[504]

Professor Saltzburg believes that trial judges are becoming more active because increasingly "lawyer error or incompetence detracts from the 'search for truth' and unfairly threatens a litigant's interest...a trial is a search for truth, not merely a battle of wits between adversaries."[505] He then quotes Judge Learned Hand who wrote that a "judge is more than a moderator; he is charged to see that the law is properly administered, and it is a duty which he cannot discharge by remaining inert."[506]

US District Judge Sam Sparks of Austin, Texas, probably would agree. When he felt that he was "not getting his message across,...he issued an order well-spiced with sarcasm, invective,

---

501. Katz, p. 102
502. Landsman, p. 77
503. Landsman, p. 32
504. Landsman, p. 32
505. Landsman, p. 117
506. Landsman, pp. 117,118

some powerful exclamations and a threat to legal fees to get the attention of lawyers he felt were trying harder to attack each other than litigate their 20-month-old case."[507]

Lawyer Frank Baffa, former supervising judge of the Torrance, California, Superior Court, states that "it is not the function of the judge to try the bad lawyer's case for him," but he admits that a "judge is and should be allowed to intervene if a key question is not being asked by counsel, particularly in criminal cases."[508]

Judith Resnik, Professor of Law, Yale Law School, is not a particular fan of managerial judges who, she believes, already have tremendous powers. "Transforming the judge from adjudicator to manager substantially expands the opportunities for judges to use—or abuse—their power."[509] She does concede that during pretrial procedures, "privacy and informality have some genuine advantages; attorneys and judges can discuss discovery schedules and explore settlement proposals without the constraints of the formal courtroom environment." But she worries that dangers also exist since the information that the judges receive during such periods "have not been filtered by the rules of evidence."[510] In other words, she favors the adversarial process that is apt to conceal some information from the judge.

Professor Saltzburg, an avid fan of the adversarial system, does not want the trial judge to have authority to "sum up and to comment upon evidence" or in most cases to have the authority "to call and to interrogate witnesses" as this denies the right of counsel "to analyze the bias of trial participants and to meet the contentions raised by opposing counsel."[511] Professor Lon Fuller, Harvard Law School, although in favor of the US system, seemed to have a broader outlook. He registered discontent with the idea that the adversarial system required the judge to remain passive throughout the trial, acting only as an umpire. "A more active participation by the

---

507. ABA Journal eReport, August 20, 2004, p. 1
508. Journal, October 1, 1988, p. 81
509. Landsman, p. 100
510. Landsman, p. 100
511. Landsman, p. 118

judge—assuming it stops short of a prejudgment of the case itself—can therefore enhance the meaning and effectiveness of an adversary presentation."[512]

One form of judicial activism could be the use of judicial sanctions, but punishing a wrongdoer is a power that judges seldom exercise. Professor Saltzburg thinks that "courts should consider imposing sanctions directly on lawyers when the courts find certain abuses of the system...When lawyers dominate and violate the rules, courts should punish them."[513] Unfortunately, some judges do not want to go to the trouble and others might feel that sanctioning would put them in the apparent position of favoritism or controlling the outcome. Yet all judicial activism has this onus.

In effect, Judge Frankel referred to judicial activism when he wrote this.

> The judge is in familiar theory the impartial director of the trial as well as the decision-maker. The judicial umpire regulates the contest, then decides who won. The office carries in theory large powers of direction in the courtroom, mitigated and justified by entire neutrality...As for neutrality, the judges are among the species of umpires who are with some frequency drawn into the fray—unwittingly run down in the scrimmage, or actually used (or attempted to be used) in the strategies of the contestants, or choosing on their own to be embroiled. The resulting role is not quite the imperial one some have seen, but more than that of the bland umpire others perceive or desire.[514]

Judicial activism really results from the inherent powers that a trial judge has. The normal exercise of these powers is not considered judicial activism, however, but note how closely related they are as lawyer Spence discusses them.

> Juries do not decide our cases—judges do. Today, no jury is permitted to hear a case in the first place unless the trial judge permits the case to go to trial. At the close of all the evidence, the judge alone determines if the party has presented a sufficient case for the jury to hear, and if the judge decides not, the case is thrown on the judicial garbage heap. Many times I have seen the judge direct the jury to

512. Landsman, pp. 50,51
513. Landsman, p. 76
514. Landsman, p. 87

return a verdict against an injured party—to sign the verdict form as he, the judge, provides, and always jurors do as he orders. They must. The judge is the law. In every trial, civil or criminal, the judge shapes the case. Before and during the trial, the judge makes rulings that determine what procedures will be followed, what evidence will be permitted to go to the jury, what law will govern the trial, what arguments will be allowed, and how long such arguments will last. The case is no longer the parties' case but the judge's, and he will fashion the case to suit his fancy.[515]

Regardless of the judges' powers, Professor Farnsworth believes that the adversarial system of justice affects the independence of the trial judge.

The adversary rather than inquisitorial character of litigation has encouraged the opposing lawyers to act as zealous partisans in presenting their cases, has contributed to a tradition of surprise and proprietorship over witnesses and information, and has accorded a relatively passive role to the judge, who acts only as arbiter and undertakes no independent investigation.[516]

Journalist Curriden notes that judges often perceive that a witness is lying but they can do nothing about it.[517] They have no way to independently investigate and are not able to prove otherwise. In other words, judges' powers are not as omnipotent as some profess. Professor Landsman confirms this. "Adversary theory requires the judge to remain passive until the conclusion of the advocates' presentation. She is not free to conduct an independent inquiry"[518]

---

515. Spence, p. 85
516. Farnsworth, p. 97
517. Journal, June 1989, p. 55
518. Landsman, p. 25

Chapter 7. The Juries

Jury Formation

For our individual and collective safety, America's judicial system, nonadversarial or otherwise, must retain the right to jury. "Thomas Jefferson was of the opinion that the right to trial by a jury of fellow citizens was a more important safeguard of personal liberty than the right to vote. With a jury, the rights and duties of each of us will be decided by our fellow citizens, not by some bureaucrat or governmental functionary."[519] It is equally important that the chosen jury be of good character and fair-minded. So how are they chosen?

First, a pool of citizens, much greater than twelve, is selected by a clerk from such as a voter list or a property assessment list. As a prospect is randomly chosen from this pool to sit on the jury, each side has an opportunity to challenge for cause. If the cause is upheld by the court, meaning the judge, then the name is dropped. Each side also has so many peremptory challenges, meaning that no cause need be shown for removing the prospect.[520]

---

519. Lawyer, November 2003, p. 5

Lawyer Kaminer says that "the more you know...the less likely you are to end up on a jury...Litigators don't seek objective, unbiased jurors; they seek jurors who seem to harbor biases that favor their respective cases." Then she quotes Mark Twain. "The jury system was the 'most ingenious and infallible agency for defeating justice that human wisdom could contrive.' The notion that jurors should have no prior knowledge of the case they were called to decide 'compels us to swear in fools and rascals...[and] rigidly excludes honest men and men of brains.'"[521]

Judge Rothwax also quoted Mark Twain who said that "we have a jury system that is superior to any in the world, and its efficacy is only marred by the difficulty of finding twelve men every day who don't know anything and can't read."[522] The judge also quoted Oliver Wendell Holmes who said that "the man who wants a jury has a bad case."[523]

Recall what lawyer Spence, who has his own sense of humor, said about a trial being a barbarous sport that is generally won by the best players. He then quoted Robert Frost who said that "a jury consists of twelve persons chosen to decide who has the better lawyer."[524] Regardless, "once impaneled the jury is presented with all the admissible evidence and then charged to render a verdict."[525]

Juries have always had the duty of determining the facts, but originally they were constituted differently. Writer Post described them this way. "[they] consisted of witnesses who decided cases largely from their own knowledge of the events...there was no requirement that a verdict must be reached on the basis of evidence presented in court."[526]

---

520. For a more detailed description of jury selection, see Post, pp. 115, 116 and Jenkins, p .334
521. Kaminer, p. 133
522. Rothwax, p. 197
523. Rothwax, p. 197
524. Spence, p. 112
525. Landsman, p. 122
526. Post, p. 53

Lawyer Rembar described them in this fashion. "It was not the jury as we know it. It was a body of neighbors who acted on their own knowledge of the facts...They did not sit and listen to the evidence; they brought the evidence to court themselves, inside their heads. The idea of proving a case in court came later... The very thing that then was looked for in a juror is now good reason to reject him."[527]

This is the way Professor Landsman put it. "The use of jurors from the neighborhood and reliance upon each juror's personal knowledge marked early jury procedure as inquisitorial rather than adversarial. The jury did not act as a neutral and passive fact finder, but as an active and inquiring body searching for material truth. Although the jury was not by its nature intrinsically adversarial, certain of its procedures and much of its early development paved the way for the later growth of the adversary process."[528]

Lawyer Katz described first how juries were originally formed,[529] and then she described our present jury system.

> Half a millennium later, three revolutionary legal concepts had emerged. One was that a jury ought to be composed of 'legal peers,' not social elites or royal agents. Another was that jurors should either have no personal knowledge of the events and people before them or else disregard that knowledge. A final concept was that the jury should be passive prior to the start of its formal deliberations. Today, these notions have been either distorted or rendered obsolete. Jurors are now often viewed as 'representative' of social, ethnic, racial, and economic groups—which can strain the idea of 'legal peer' juries chosen from the general population. Jurors are now too often chosen and valued, not for their knowledge or their impartiality, but for their ignorance and their prejudices. And finally, the requirement for passivity, which bars the jury from seeking the kinds of information it needs to do its decision-making job, exacerbates the effects of ignorance and prejudice...In short, without decision-makers who possess or can acquire adequate information, 21st century civil justice cannot and will not work.[530]

---

527. Rembar, p. 129
528. Landsman, p. 9
529. Katz, p. 97
530. Katz, pp. 97,98

Judge Rothwax took up the requirement of unanimity of the jurors. "The necessity of unanimity from twelve jurors has continued to be a source of frustration in the court's ability to carry out justice...the US Constitution does not require unanimous verdicts...[but] It's a sacred cow."[531] However, that is not quite true, as the US Supreme Court has held in at least two cases that unanimity is "not required in state court criminal trials."[532] Yet, "An ABA project to revamp jury standards has proposed a return to 12-person, unanimous juries."[533]

Section 2 of Article III of the US Constitution, which pertains to federal crimes, states that "the trial of all Crimes...shall be by Jury" and Amendment VI, which pertains to state crimes, says that "in all criminal prosecutions, the accused shall enjoy the right to...an impartial jury." Relative to the latter, Judge Rothwax had this to say. "Although the Sixth Amendment requires an 'impartial' jury, we have ceased in this day and age to believe in impartiality. And lawyers don't necessarily even want it."[534] Amendment VII gives the right to a jury trial. "In suits at common law [i.e., civil suits], where the value in controversy shall exceed twenty dollars"

Former Chief US District Judge for Minnesota Edward J. Devitt, now deceased, would have liked this provision amended,[535] presumably to set a much higher amount. Fortunately, the legal profession has not burdened the courts with the foolishness of asking for a jury in such a small amount, or even with suing for that amount. In any event, the use of a jury is not automatic. "Generally, the litigant has some choice. In civil cases, a jury will not be called unless one side or the other asks for it; in criminal cases the accused may waive a jury."[536]

As especially noted during the O. J. Simpson era, jurors and jury panels are professionally screened, at least for the "big" trials.

---

531. Rothwax, pp. 211,213
532. Landsman, pp. 23,166
533. Journal, December 2004, p. 62
534. Rothwax, p. 204
535. Landsman, p. 147
536. Rembar, p. 336

"The principal objective for both sides: flush out and eliminate unsympathetic jurors."[537] What is the effect? "Some legal analysts worry that the jury system wasn't designed to withstand this kind of skillful manipulation. 'It just pushes us very far away from the concept of the jury being a cross-section of the community, says Stephen Adler, author.'"[538] This would not be a problem if the adversarial system were done away with, since in that event both sides would be searching for the truth, not merely seeking victory by manipulating the jury selection.

In the meantime, lawyers are in court not to lose but to win. "Jury selection has become too much of a competition between sides rather than simply finding a fair and impartial jury," according to University of Georgia law Professor Ronald L. Carlson.[539] Attorneys will continue to use their rights to peremptory challenges and challenges for cause in order to gain juries most favorable to their clients' causes. The federal courts do have one advantage over most state courts. There, the judges do the "grilling," not the attorneys.[540]

Judge Rothwax has this to say about a jury.

> The jury is considered the jewel and the centerpiece of the American criminal justice system. It represents the people standing between a possibly oppressive government and the lonely, accused individual...When we say that our system is the best in the world, we generally have the jury in mind...The rhetoric that idealizes the jury and the reality of its operation are in conflict...Although attorneys and judges will often proclaim their admiration of a jury's ability to reach the truth, privately they will acknowledge that a trial before a jury is a crapshoot, a roll of the dice, with all the randomness and uncertainty that implies. To some extent this is a product of the exclusionary rules and rules of evidence...But to a greater extent it is a comment on the procedures by which we recruit and select jurors, and the way that we manipulate them, orient them, instruct them, and condition their behavior.[541]

---

537. *Newsweek*, August 22, 1994, p. 29
538. *Newsweek*, August 22, 1994, p. 29
539. Journal, November 1995, p. 74
540. Gazette, June 27, 1993, p. 1B
541. Rothwax, pp. 199, 200

Actually, Judge Rothwax could have said that the way American juries are manipulated is the result of the adversarial system, since under our present system rarely do both sides want to determine the truth. One party, or maybe both parties, will not be anxious to suffer a jury that tries to find, or is even able to find, the truth. In spite of all that has been said herein, however, jurors, if given the chance, often seem to find the truth, in spite of our archaic procedures and questionable tactics by one or both parties.

That juries are manipulated, not to find the truth but to favor one or the other parties, cannot be denied. On May 11, 2006, this writer received an email from Audio@ConstitutionConferences.com on the subject "Last Chance for Strategic Jury Selection: Keys to Winning Your Case." The email stated that "Jury selection is a process that is both a science and an art." Among the subjects were "Keys to identifying jurors who will respond favorable to your case [and] Designing questions for strategic advantage." Obviously, a crafty trial lawyer's aim is to win, not to find the truth, certainly not for the jury to determine the truth.

Robert J. Grey Jr., 2004-2005 ABA President, made it a point to address jury issues, hoping for improvement of the system including its operations, composition, comprehension, and convenience.[542] Due to his efforts, a jury project was instigated. For more details concerning what has resulted, see Chapter 9.

THE JURORS' VIEWPOINT

> Juries...perform the function that the law assigns to them. The jury hears the testimony of the witnesses, evaluates the evidence, determines the facts, applies to those facts the law as given by the judge, and reaches what is called a "general verdict." In a criminal case, after deliberation, the jury finds the accused "guilty" or "not guilty"; in a civil case, "We find for the plaintiff in the sum of" or "We find for the defendants." The jury does not have to explain the verdict; it merely states a conclusion.[543]

542. Journal, August 2004, p. 58
543. Post, p. 127

That is supposedly the orderly procedure that juries follow, but lawyer Kaminer thinks otherwise. "Jurors not only make their sentencing decision at the wrong stage of the trial, before they have heard all the evidence, they tend to be swayed by factors that are not legally relevant, such as a defendant's silence when given a chance to testify or a defendant's courtroom demeanor."[544] Others might agree. "Most of what the jury picks up is what people are *doing*. Not what they're saying. Only a small part is picked up through the spoken word."[545]

According to writer Post, "today, there is doubt as to its [the jury's] usefulness; there is more than a suggestion that trial by jury has passed its prime; that it is deficient as a mode of resolving conflicts fairly and honestly."[546] What those critics do not seem to understand is that it is not the jury that is at fault. It is the form of justice that we maintain and tolerate. When the lawyers do not deal with the truth fairly and honestly, even conscientious juries cannot determine what is true. According to Miami lawyer Ellis Rubin, "jury trials today are no longer a search for truth, but a gigantic lying contest...They are a crime scene."[547] This will be the situation as long as we tolerate the adversarial form to obtain the truth, or simply to hide the truth.

Trial lawyer Knight explains the dilemma of the jurors.

> They are, in fact, asked to do superhuman things—things we know they cannot, and do not, do. They are asked to wipe from their minds testimony they were not supposed to have heard; resolve conflicts in evidence no mortal could resolve with any confidence; identify thoughts that flickered through the consciousness of people at precise moments months and years in the past; absorb and apply pages of complex instructions concerning legal principles they have never heard of. And in reaching a verdict, they are asked to perform a feat of probably impossible schizophrenia: If they *believe* the defendant is guilty, they must nonetheless find that he is *not* if they have a reasonable doubt that he *is*. Each of them must find a way to agree

---

544. Kaminer, p. 145
545. Jenkins, p. 293
546. Post, p. 127
547. Journal, August 1, 1987, p. 29

with eleven random strangers on this elusive, difficult proposition, or their labors are in vain.[548]

Judge Jerome New Frank, who died while serving on the US Court of Appeals for the Second Circuit, once said that "we tell jurors to do—have them take an oath to do—what we do not at all expect them to do."[549] Professor Maechling gives his impression of the jury. "Deprived of a great deal of relevant information, and forced by the rules to receive what is deemed admissible in piecemeal form removed from real-life context, the jury is required to determine guilt or innocence on the narrowest grounds possible."[550]

Another group of writers claims that the jury system is inefficient, but in the same breath perhaps explains why. "The jury system is inefficient—and mistreats those it calls upon for help. Jurors must make excruciatingly difficult decisions, but are given only garbled legalistic instructions and are strictly prohibited from taking an active part in trials."[551]

Writer Post explains what happens when testimony is conflicting.

> One might think that where the testimony of witnesses for both sides conflicts as to the essential points of a case, the jury would reach an impasse. Yet such conflict of testimony does not, as a matter of law, give rise to a reasonable doubt; nor does it require the court to discharge the defendant on the ground of insufficient evidence. The jury should attempt to reconcile such conflicting evidence as much as possible, since it is presumed that the witnesses are honest. If the testimony cannot be reconciled, the jury must then decide who is to be believed and who is not.[552]

That really reveals the vagaries of the adversarial system, a system that encourages the one guilty or the one liable to sow confusion in the minds of the jurors.

Despite these many sympathetic observations of the jurors, Franklin Delano Strier, Professor of Accounting and Law, California

---

548. Knight, pp. 253,254
549. Landsman, p. 144
550. Journal, January 1991, p. 60
551. Elias, p. 61
552. Post, p. 132

State University at Dominguez Hills, Carson, California, himself observed that "yet, surprisingly little has been done to investigate the perceptions of *actual* jurors. What do they think of the trial process, of the lawyers' tactics? How do those perceptions affect a jury's decisions?"[553]

One poll of jurors indicated that many "respondents spot attorney mischief. About two-fifths felt 'one or both attorneys were trying more to distort or selectively hide facts rather than seeking to reveal the truth so the jury could make an informed judgment.'"[554] Judge Frank suggested that once the trial begins, judges do not really want to delve into the workings and minds of the jurors. "The judges feel that, were they obliged to learn the methods used by juror, the actual workings of the jury-system would be shown up, devastatingly. From my point of view, such a consequence would be desirable: The public would soon discover this skeleton in the judicial closet."[555]

In an article on medical malpractice claims, it was asserted that "juries...have great difficulty deciding very complicated and emotional cases."[556] That should be no surprise under the US system of justice. Jury participation in the trial may be an answer to some of the jury confusion. One possible remedy is to allow jurors to take notes. "Those jurors who commented on their note-taking experience said that it helped them remember witness testimony, provided a way of checking details, allowed them to better organize information and assisted their decision making."[557]

The ABA jury project mentioned in the previous chapter also proposes that jurors be allowed to take notes and "in civil cases, questions from jurors,"[558] which is allowed now in a limited number of jurisdictions. Because of the adversarial system, both of those proposals make trial lawyers extremely nervous, as does the proposal

---

553. Journal, October 1, 1988, p. 79
554. Journal, October 1, 1988, p. 80
555. Landsman, p. 140
556. Journal, March 1, 1988, p. 48
557. Journal, March 1, 1986, p. 21
558. Journal, December 2004, p. 62

that jurors be allowed to discuss the testimony prior to the conclusion of the trial.

Although these notions are not popular with many trial
lawyers, imagine, for example, college students who want to be successful attending class and never taking notes, never asking questions, or never discussing what they have learned. Judges also have
their concerns. "The current lack of guidelines dissuades many
judges from using innovative jury procedures because they fear
being reversed."[559]

Regardless of arguments for jury reform, jurors themselves
"fear they will make a serious mistake—do an injustice because they
were led astray by some tricky lawyer."[560] Judge Neely confirms
this. "An American jury is a wonder to behold. Ordinary citizens
who serve on juries are careful that they do not convict an innocent
person."[561] In a way, lawyer John A. Jenkins, who quotes lawyer
Philip H. Corboy, additionally confirms this. "I have what jurors
want. They want charisma. They want a fight in the courtroom.
They don't want placidity. They don't want a one-dimensional
lawsuit. They came here for a show! And they want to do what's
right."[562]

These accolades of jurors may be a bit overdone, according to
Judge Posner, who said that "the fact that juries, unlike judges, do
not give any justification for their decisions is a dead giveaway; a
requirement that jurors explain their votes would be a source of
profound embarrassment to the legal system."[563]

More than an embarrassment according to lawyer F. Lee
Bailey who said that if a record of jury's deliberations were made,
"we in the profession [would be] terrified of what such a record
might reveal"[564] Perhaps jury misconduct, if any, results from the
general principle, with exceptions, that a jury is always right, never

---

559. Journal, December 1989, p. 36
560. Journal, March 1996, p. 87
561. Neely, p. 126
562. Jenkins, p. 315
563. Posner, p. 209
564. *Newsweek*, January 2, 1978, p. 7

wrong, a principle that has historic beginnings according to lawyer Alfred H. Knight. "The verdict in a case is the exclusive province of the jury...It is what the jury says it is, nothing more, nothing less, and nothing different, and jurors may not be coerced into agreeing with the court's view, or punished for concluding otherwise."[565]

The exceptions to this general principle are that a judge may "take the case away from the jury by granting a motion for a directed verdict or for judgment notwithstanding the verdict."[566] And, of course, a successful appeal may effectively take the case away from the jury.

According to Professor Strier, "A perception that attorneys manipulate jurors can also reflect negatively on the trial court system. As one juror observed, 'The adversary system is a poor way of reaching the truth.'"[567] That juror was truly observant, but perhaps most jurors are. Lawyer Spence seems to understand why our system is so poor. "How can the jury do justice when it is never permitted to know all the facts?"[568]

THE PERCEPTION OF JURORS

Lawyer Kagan quotes Albert Alschuler who wrote that "the American jury trial...has become one of the most cumbersome and expensive fact-finding mechanisms that humankind has devised."[569] She then explains why. "The expansion of the American criminal trial springs from the intensification of adversarial legalism."[570] Kagan offers further arguments.

> By making litigation and adjudication slow, very costly, and unpredictable, adversarial legalism often transforms the civil justice

---

565. Knight, p. 253
566. Posner, p. 208
567. Journal, October 1, 1988, p. 80
568. Spence, p. 183
569. Kagan, p. 82
570. Kagan, p. 82

system into an engine of injustice, compelling litigants to abandon just claims and defenses.[571]

In the jury system judgment is entrusted to an ever-changing cluster of individuals who are not told about the applicable rules of law until the trial is over, nor instructed how similar cases have been decided by other juries. Jurors are not expected to explain and justify their decisions, and thus one jury's decisions cannot be systematically compared with another's.[572]

The system of justice rests on the sanctity of the jury room. Jurors are supposed to do their job with a clean slate, judging a case solely on the evidence produced in the courtroom . . . . Society...reposes its trust—and authority—in jurors to render legal decisions on its behalf.[573]

This is true even though Judge Rothwax said that "a jury trial is a crapshoot."[574] This cannot be otherwise when "the deciders, though commissioned to discover the truth, are passive recipients, not active explorers."[575]

This enforced passiveness creates a harmful attitude among jurors, one of whom described jury trials as, "archaic and unfair."[576] Judge Frank believes that the exclusionary rules of evidence were "perpetuated primarily because of the admitted incompetence of jurors."[577] Lawyer Rembar called the jurors "a group of amateurs."[578] An English barrister described a jury as "twelve people of average ignorance."[579] Would jurors, however, be as incompetent as described, if all the facts are presented to them fairly in logical order and they are given the opportunity to be active in some form? Lawyer Crier wrote that "it is ridiculous that we expect these people [the jurors] to make life-and-death decisions but are afraid to give them all the facts."[580]

---

571. Kagan, p. 117
572. Kagan, p. 114
573. Journal, August 1992, p.48
574. Rothwax, p. 162
575. Landsman, p. 55
576. Journal, October 1, 1988, p. 81
577. Landsman, p. 144
578. Rembar, p. 228. See also, Friedman(2), p. 288
579. Bugliosi, p. 56

According to one study of juries, "something like 30 percent of the public [have] no confidence in the jury system."[581] Observing the O. J. Simpson trial was a revelation to much of the public. "Many members of the public were appalled by what they learned during jury selection. First, they thought the process took too long. Second, many saw the use of jury consultants by both sides as a blatant attempt to tilt the system. The feeling is that deceit played a greater role in the selection than a real desire to obtain impartial jurors."[582] Saul M. Kassin, Professor of Psychology at Williams College, Williamstown, Massachusetts, and Lawrence S. Wrightsman, Professor of Psychology at University of Kansas, question "whether the system of justice is served by opposing attorneys trying to pick the most biased jury possible."[583] No thinking person should doubt that statement.

Judge Frank discussed "the difficulty jurors have in comprehending the evidence...the evidence is not presented all at once or in an orderly fashion. The very mode of its presentation is confusing. The jurors are supposed to keep their minds in suspense until all of the evidence is in."[584] Lawyer Katz discusses the jury's dilemma in making a decision when receiving contradictory testimony.

> In theory, the adversary system requires that the decision-makers know only what is properly presented to them. The parties-in-interest and their counsel provide the witnesses, exhibits, and documentation...expert witnesses may be used to introduce and express opinions on the evidence...And therein lies the problem. An entire industry of hired-gun experts, whose testimony is more-or-less expert but also clearly partisan, has arisen...So the decision-makers are left once again with little substance and lots of raw adversarial process, which the opposing lawyers then try to exploit for their own purposes.[585]

580. Crier, p. 214
581. Journal, June 1995, p. 32
582. Journal, June 1995, p. 75
583. Journal, July 1, 1988, p. 110
584. Landsman, p. 141
585. Katz, pp. 104,105

Lack of cooperation between the opposing attorneys creates this confusion. It is highly conceivable, of course, that at least one of the opposing attorneys relishes, in fact encourages, the resultant muddle.

Strangely, the presiding judge does not instruct the jurors until all the evidence is in. "For the first time, are the jurors asked to consider the testimony in the light of the rules. In other words, if jurors are to do their duty, they must now recollect and assemble the separate fragments of the evidence (including the demeanor of the several witnesses) and fit them into the rules."[586] This occurs after at least one of the attorneys has made every effort to suppress or distort the truth. Yet, a poor decision is blamed on the jurors, not on the adversarial system.

A few jurors come away from their experience stating it was fun, but it is doubtful that a truly conscientious person would so describe their time on the jury. "The jury system probably demands more of people than they can be expected to deliver, especially under stress. Jury service is, after all, an ordeal, It's often uncomfortable and unpleasant...[jurors] feel the burden of passing judgment on people"[587] *Newsweek*, in its *Conventional Wisdom* column, gave a thumbs down on juries. "Trial by peers? More like trial by fears. Try listening to judges' instructions."[588]

Judge Frank is quoted as saying that juries "have again and again arrived at a verdict by one of two or three methods: (1) in a civil case, each juror writes down the amount of money he wants to award the plaintiff; the total is added and the average taken as the verdict; (2) the jurors, by agreement, decide for one side or the other of a civil case by flipping a coin; and (3) the jurors decide by majority vote, after previous agreement to do so."[589] Writer Post states that conclusions reached by a jury "are usually conclusions of probability, not of certainty."[590] Judge Neely believes that "jury caprice

586. Landsman, p. 142
587. Kaminer, p. 146
588. *Newsweek*, December 26, 1994/January 2, 1995, p. 17
589. Post, p. 129. See also, Landsman, p. 139
590. Post, p. 130

causes most people to insure against judges and juries, not against their own negligence."[591]

America's doctors of medicine apparently do not like the adversarial system of justice. "In the adversarial system, physicians believe they're just getting the best presentation instead of getting to the truth."[592] Donald J. Palmisano, past president of the AMA and holder of a J.D., has been quoted as saying that "it may not be a bad idea to do away with the jury system further down the road."[593] These kinds of thought are scary but they will gain traction if the adversarial system and its twin, the attorney-client privilege, are not done away with. Unfortunately, the general public, even some lawyers, cannot comprehend the inherent problems in our jury system, as does lawyer Katz who wrote this.

> When jurors cannot grasp the evidence, they have scant recourse save to base their decisions on criteria having little or nothing to do with the dispute at hand—criteria such as race, gender, the lawyers' theatrics, even their (and their clients') clothing or hair. If jurors vote on the basis of purely personal preferences or subcultural affiliation because they are unable to vote on the basis of the evidence, then the very diversity that could be a source of strength becomes a curse, undermining the jury's vital role within the adversary system. The goal must be diverse juries that can evaluate the evidence objectively and decide accordingly.[594]

Lawyer Rembar expended some time critiquing the jury, he believing it was wise to continue its use in criminal cases but not in civil cases.[595] Actually, it is the lawyers' misuse of the jury and the consequences of the adversarial system that should be criticized, not the jury itself. Even so, critical comments concerning juries, as if they were the reason for problems in our judicial system, continue unabated. "Across the nation, there are calls to reform the jury system."[596] After the O. J. Simpson trial, David A. Kaplan, Senior

---

591. Neely, p. 110
592. Journal, March 2005, p. 40
593. Journal, March 2005, p. 42
594. Katz, pp. 121,122
595. Rembar, pp. 335,336
596. Journal, November 1995, p. 72

Writer in *Newsweek*, questioned, "Is the American jury an anachronism, an institution that no longer works in the day of jury consultants, complex scientific testimony and racial polarization among diverse juries?"[597] It seems odd that critics and reformers choose to pick on the jury rather than on the adversarial system. Apparently, though, the adversarial system itself is even more sacrosanct than the jury.

Perhaps Judge Rothwax touches upon the truth, the reason why juries appear to be unreliable and incompetent. "If we had complete faith in the ability of the jury to function as mature, sophisticated, and intelligent fact finders, then we could submit to them *all* relevant evidence, but we don't have that faith...We are forever shielding the tender eyes of the jury from the harsh realities of the truth. Because we do not trust the jury to sift that which is probative from that which is prejudicial, we exclude relevant evidence from the jury when the judge concludes that the prejudicial impact of the evidence exceeds its probative value. Sometimes even when the evidence is *highly* probative, it is excluded because it is 'too inflammatory.'"[598]

Not all courts mistrust the jurors. "Jurors are being asked to participate actively in proceedings...by allowing jurors to take notes...submit written questions to the bench—or even question witnesses directly."[599] Needless to say, "[trial lawyers] greet the jury reforms with trepidation, if not outright hostility."[600] That should come as no surprise in view of the US system. Robert W. Landry, formerly judge of the Milwaukee County Circuit Court, was a great fan of an active jury. "The justice system should be based on the truth, and the search for justice is not aided by limits on finding the truth."[601]

---

597. *Newsweek*, October 16, 1995, p. 58
598. Rothwax, pp. 208-210
599. *Newsweek*, August 7, 1989, p. 51
600. *Newsweek*, August 7, 1989, p. 51
601. *Parade*, August 27, 1989, p. 8

On a more positive note, "The Iowa experience is that juries tend to be fair and impartial and return verdicts that are consistent with the evidence."[602]

---

602. Lawyer, November 2003, p. 4

Chapter 8. Reform

Katz made several comments relative to reform of our legal system.

> As Americans have come to demand more of their legal system, they have also come to have less faith in its fairness. And cosmetic or peripheral reforms cannot begin to restore either the system's fairness or the citizenry's faith.[603]

> Our quest for justice may be sacred. Our civil justice system, in its present form, is not. It can and must be changed. It is a system instituted by the American Founders and modified by their descendants to handle day-to-day problems. As these problems change, the problem-solving system must also change if it is to continue to fulfill its function. Given the immensity of the changes coming upon us, tepid and half-hearted tinkering will not be enough, and may indeed lead to a misplaced and potentially disastrous sense of false security. We must stop pretending, denying, and protesting when it comes to legal reform....We must start thinking and acting.[604]

According to *Newsweek*, "legal reform is a painfully slow process."[605] Reform may be slow but that does not mean that it

---

603. Katz, p. 31
604. Katz, p. 153

should not be attempted. Judge Horn writes that "expert opinion...collectively suggest troubling trends in the legal profession. Some commentators, particularly those writing from the academy, see the profession as dying, as 'on the edge of chaos,' or otherwise as being in extremis."[606] That statement itself may be extreme, but for some reason not entirely clear judicial indicters shy away from the antidotes, drastic as they might seem to them, that are necessary to properly reform the system of justice.

Quite unfortunately, suggested legal reform today has too narrow a focus. The same article in *Newsweek* seems to confirm this when it stated that "conventional tort reform does not really go at the deeper problem. It does not bring about fundamental change in a system that affects the lives of millions by disrupting the services they depend on."[607] Doing what is advocated in this book would solve the alleged tort reform problems, but tort reform is not the whole picture. Think of criminal trials, for instance. They are at least as important as civil cases.

And think of the behavior of trial lawyers, or at least some of them. And how many trial judges have the wit to do what King County, Washington, Superior Court Judge Suzanne M. Barnett did. Finding that a Seattle law firm violated one of its civil rules, by making eight claims in a counterclaim that were deemed without merit, she assessed the firm $400,000 in sanctions.[608]

More than a decade ago, then ABA President Ide made these observations.

> All of our institutions are facing new and greater demands...No institution is more profoundly affected by these changes than our justice system. Yet, it has been the slowest to recognize the importance of adapting...our justice system is still plodding along using early 20th century techniques and, in too many cases, reverting to 19th century attitudes about the meaning of dispensing justice. As we move into the next century, it is essential for us to retool our justice system so that the 21st century will be one of real justice.[609]

605. *Newsweek*, December 15, 2003, p. 51
606. Horn, p. 78
607. *Newsweek*, December 15, 2003, p. 51
608. ABA Journal eReport, November 21, 2003, p. 1

In his commentary, Ide did not mention our archaic adversarial system. Unlike some judges and a few law professors, bar
leaders treat the system of justice as untouchable, apparently no
matter what they think of it. Just a year or so previously, Judge
Neely had written this.

> Superimposing twentieth-century problems on a medieval struc-
> ture for handling them means increasing deterioration of the effec-
> tiveness of the courts. The question of overall design implies new
> ways of handling old controversies that may affect their outcome—
> winners may become losers. It is for this reason that there is so little
> innovation. If the courts become more efficient, and therefore benefit
> one group, then adjustments must be made in the design to compen-
> sate other groups that had derived advantages from inefficiency.[610]

In some ways, that is a dismal statement for anyone who
desires to reform the system of justice. Increasingly, however,
appear signs of discontent with our judicial system, some of which,
as already indicated, are rather narrow in content. For instance, columnist Samuelson, the non-practicing lawyer who is an admitted
lawyer-basher, has touted "the English rule. It requires the losing
side in a civil suit to pay the winning side's attorneys' costs."[611] One
wonders whether elimination of the adversarial system would make
the English rule unnecessary in his eyes.

Although nothing much came of it, the Simpson trial evoked
many comments about the need to change the system. This one
appeared in the *ABA Journal*.

> For better or worse, the Simpson case is now part of our culture,
> along with a magnified sense that something is seriously wrong with
> our justice system as demonstrated by the circus-like atmosphere of
> the trial...[quoting Professor Langbein]: "It's the first time a large por-
> tion of the thinking populace has come to see how dysfunctional and
> truth-defeating our criminal trial procedure really is."[612]

Even though few would argue with that, on the other hand
few have done anything to try to remedy the situation, even after a

---

609. Journal, January 1994, p. 6
610. Neely, p. 11
611. *Newsweek*, April 27, 1992, p. 62
612. Journal, November 1995, p. 48c

scathing, award-winning article about the legal system that was written by Alexandria, Virginia, lawyer John W. Toothman for the *ABA Journal.*

There is the need to avoid the detours taken by others through substantive and procedural reforms.... Any improvement upon the justice system must be accomplished with relative neutrality or else the entire system will ebb and flow with each political sea change.... Because they are implemented in an adversarial system, changes in procedural rules, even facially neutral ones, either have surprisingly little impact or only serve to complicate rather than simplify the system.

The reason these reforms derailed is that lawyers, claiming a duty of zealous representation but who are motivated by a desire to run up fees, always can find something to argue about.... The result, by virtue of the adversarial process, is that no procedural change is ever the last word and nothing is ever final. Thus, any real reform must take this dynamic into account or else be doomed.

Bluntly put, hourly billing and the duty of zealous representation—two self-constructed pillars of the legal profession sacrosanct to most lawyers—are responsible for spiraling costs and delays. Avoid them, and the path to justice would be cheaper and quicker. Billing requirements and zealous advocacy provide a motivation and a justification for running up legal costs and delay.

Some litigators cannot conceive of handling a case without the usual overstaffing and overkill in motion practice, discovery and wrangling with opposing counsel.... When pressed to justify their expensive strategies and tactics, law firms invariably take shelter behind the pillar of zealous representation.

Generations of litigators have put the duty of zealous representation on a pedestal.... The irony is that zealousness was supposed to protect clients, not punish them.

Zeal, divorced from sensitivity to cost and delay, has harmed the very clients whose interests were the justification for this extraordinary duty in the first place.... Lawyers must be reminded, and clients reassured, that a zealous adversarial position may be reached by many paths, with the quickest and cheapest having the advantage of better serving a client's financial interest.... In the end, the notion that some lawyers may opt out of reform is illusory.[613]

---

613. Journal, September 1995, pp.80-83

Professor Hazard exhibits considerable wistfulness when he speaks of the English barrister. "The advocate undertakes a dispassionate analysis of the facts and a magisterial consideration of the law with the aim of establishing common ground with his opposite number and thereupon settling the case on the basis of truth and legal justice, or at worst, isolating for trial the issues of fact or law that prove intractable. A lot of litigation in this country is actually determined this way, when the advocates trust each other's competence, integrity, and judgment. But a lot of litigation is conducted otherwise. In the other approach, the advocate is a street fighter— aggressive, guileful, exploitive."[614] The latter is bound to exist when the *ABA Model Rules of Professional Conduct* allow such shameful conduct on the excuse that lawyers should be "zealous" in their representation and lawyers plead fear of malpractice if they aren't zealous.

Lawyer Spence believes that the system must devise a better way to ascertain the facts. When he says "facts," doesn't he really mean "truth"? He describes the problem as "one of the great challenges of our justice system."[615] Judge Neely underscores the problems of change. "Most active members of institutionalized 'law reform' groups, particularly the bar associations, are lawyers who have devoted their lives to mastering the current system...law, after all, is a profession that is usually chosen for its financial rewards. In the final analysis, thinking about reform of the total system is both financially and academically unrewarding."[616] With considerable insight, Judge Neely has more to say.

> When we think in terms of court reform, we must think of designing systems that will keep people out of court rather than giving them a better result once they are in court...all procedures concerning litigation should always take into consideration how in-court procedures can lead to equitable out-of-court settlements...We need a system that at every point is designed not to process litigation but to reduce the need for litigation at all. If every time an appellate court wrote an opinion all the judges devoted fifteen minutes to asking

---

614. Landsman, p. 203
615. Spence, p. 269
616. Neely, p. 61

themselves how the new ruling could be molded to make settlements easier, within about ten years the system would be dramatically improved.[617]

No one who wants reform believes that it will come easily. Observe writer Olson. "There is, in short, no easy way to avoid the task of bringing sense back to our legal system. Litigation must be reformed from within, by rolling back the powers of imposition that make it so fearful."[618] The following passages from an article written by Professor Maechling indicate the difficulties, but also the possibilities, of reforming at least a portion of our judicial system.

> Whether the deficiencies of the American adversarial method can be rectified is an open question. Indeed, at first glance, the US Constitution and Bill of Rights do appear to raise insuperable barriers to change. But closer examination will reveal that many of the anachronisms [of our judicial system]...are not anchored in the specific language of the Constitution. They either are the product of later interpretation by the Supreme Court or derive from British precedents...For example:

> There is nothing in the Bill of Rights that requires that evidence procured in violation of the Fourth Amendment prohibition against unreasonable searches and seizures be inadmissible in court. To the contrary, the early history of this provision indicates that it was designed to protect private property and the integrity of the home... rather than to interfere with the prosecution of criminals. The exclusionary rule in federal courts dates back only to 1914, and in state courts to...1961.

> The Fifth Amendment prohibition against self-incrimination could be restored by the Supreme Court to its declared purpose of preventing self-incrimination in a criminal case against the accused, and removed as an excuse for allowing a defendant to evade truthful responses in congressional inquiries and other forums.

> The archaic rule against admission of hearsay evidence—the kind of information governments and ordinary people use daily to make decisions—finds no mention in the Constitution and could be eliminated at a stroke by legislative fiat.

> The Sixth Amendment requirement of impartiality (of jurors) need not be a mandate for political illiteracy.

---

617. Neely, pp. 123,124
618. Olson, p. 313

There is also no reason why all witnesses in a criminal trial—especially 'expert' witnesses picked for their biases and coached to give slanted testimony—should not be witnesses for the court, selected and screened for competence and objectivity. Or why most of the questioning of witnesses should not be the function of the judge, with the lawyers only permitted a limited right of final questioning.[619]

Professor Landsman is a fan of the adversarial process, although he correctly articulates what is usually considered bad about the system. Here, in part, is what he wrote.

The three facets of the adversary system most strongly condemned as inhibitors of the discovery of truth are party control of the information-gathering process, zealous and single-minded representation of each litigant by his attorney, and evidentiary rules that circumscribe the types of information available to the decision maker...[but] it need not be conceded that the process is inept at finding truth.

To become preoccupied with truth may be both naïve and futile. It is to the advantage of the adversary system that it does not define its objectives in such an absolute and unrealistic fashion...a preoccupation with material truth may be not only futile but dangerous to society as well. If the exclusive objective of the judicial process were the disclosure of facts, then any technique that increases the prospect of gathering facts would be permissible.

Truth is not the end the courts seek. Truth is nothing more than a means of achieving the end, justice. The disclosure of material facts is not the only means of achieving justice, and to treat it as the end is to open the way to unsavory abuses. Critics of the adversary system argue that parties should not be allowed to control the information-gathering process because they cannot be trusted to present all the relevant evidence. Rather, the parties are likely to provide only the information that they think helps their cause. This sort of presentation is said to skew the proof in ways that undermine the accuracy of the final determination...In response it should be remarked that party control is necessary to preserve the neutrality of the fact finder.[620]

Some response needs to be made to all that lawyer-talk that fogs the issue. For some reason, or maybe it is obvious why, proponents of the adversarial system object strenuously to equating the

---

619. Journal, January 1991, pp. 62,63
620. Landsman, pp. 26-28

system with truth. First, as did Professor Landsman, they deny that truth cannot be found in the system and then, regardless they say, truth is not all that important, that there are other considerations as, or more, important than the truth.

These proponents of adversaryism don't seem to realize that failure to secure the truth could result in conviction of the innocent as well as the guilty. The purpose of a trial is to seek the truth; it should not be otherwise. But the fact finder may not be able to discern the truth if one of the parties is obscuring it. Judge Fleming may be referring to the latter when he remarked that "disruptive tendencies [are] latent in the adversary judicial process."[621]

Not so latent, perhaps, during the Simpson trial. A poll taken during that trial revealed that the great majority believed that "the evidentiary waters are muddied to the point where the truth can no longer be discerned, justice cannot be done."[622] In other words, justice without truth is no justice at all. Andree Seu, senior writer for World magazine, presumably would agree. "Things work when they are based on truth."[623]

Due to his experience as Chief Justice of West Virginia, Judge Neely is pessimistic about fixing a "broken machine." He believes that the "political process is paralyzed by a web of vested interests, many of which profit from the current disorder in the courts." He further believes that "all proposals for reforms predicated on the supposition that expanding personnel, streamlining procedure, or increasing the number of courts will cure the courts' problems are naïve and doomed to failure. The fact is that courts don't work because at some point in the system most people consciously, and deliberately, do not want them to work...In order to make any major improvement in the way courts perform, it is necessary to think creatively about some entirely new designs, not about bigger and better versions of our current obsolete design."[624]

---

621. Fleming, p. 170
622. Journal, June 1995, p. 78
623. World, January 31, 2004, p. 43
624. Neely, pp. 7-9

Professor Landsman thinks, however, that "the chief justification for change has been the claimed need for greater speed and efficiency."[625] To the contrary, although speed and efficiency may, and probably would, result, the chief reason for eliminating the adversarial process is to make it probable, not merely possible, that the parties that should succeed do in fact succeed and that the parties that should lose do in fact lose.

Judge Neely, while discussing the issue of allocating costs of litigation, makes the following observation. "Settlement [of a suit or claim] is really what civilization in general and courts in particular should be about."[626] Doing away with the adversarial process would greatly enhance settlement and, even more so, constrain otherwise frivolous lawsuits. Actually, a combination of assigning costs and inability to use the shifty adversarial process would do wonders in decreasing the number of potential lawsuits. If so, would even starving lawyers take on meritless cases, when the absence of the adversarial process would give them little hope of success and saddle them or their clients with the legal costs?

POSITION OF THE BAR

In November 2004, the Iowa State Bar Association conducted "an intense workshop on direct and cross-examination of witnesses for prosecutors and defense counsel who need concentrated training on those fine and subtle arts."[627] That is quite embarrassing that lawyers need training in finding the truth in the courtroom. The legal training really should be to teach lawyers how to wring out the truth from their own clients. Otherwise, a system that requires opposing counsel to determine the truth perpetuates a bad situation.

---

625. Landsman, p. 106
626. Neely, p. 185
627. Lawyer, January 2005, p. 7

Listen again to Judge Rothwax as he described our present system of justice.

> The role of the defense attorney is to zealously represent his client within the bounds of the law, to defend his client whether he is guilty or not guilty, and so to attack the accusing witnesses whatever the truth of those accusations may be. But can we conceive—and *should* we conceive—of a system in which defense attorneys would be more willing to view themselves as part of a system of law, and less willing to see themselves as the alter ego of their client?[628]

Any change will be difficult because of the stakes in the present system. As reported in World magazine, trials are big business; they generate more revenue than either Pfizer or Microsoft. "Of the $200 billion generated by lawsuits each year, almost 20 percent goes to the lawyers who brought the suits."[629] Perhaps unfortunately for the legal profession as a whole, the same article states that the trial lawyers "may be the most influential legal group in America."[630] Professor Langbein tells why. "There is one great set of winners in American criminal justice: the lawyers. Now grown immensely wealthy and powerful, the elite criminal bar constitutes an entrenched vested interest for the perpetuation of our failed system."[631] Judge Rothwax explained.

> Those working within the system are self-interested or have institutional interests they are determined to defend. They are often quick to question the motives, values, or competence of those who would challenge things as they are. Some principles, procedures, and practices are held to be sacrosanct.... When dissident voices are raised, there is a concerted cacophony that is quick to question their motives and values.[632]

Professor Landsman somehow feels that under an inquisitorial judicial system the "judge will abandon neutrality if encouraged to search for material truth and...the attorney will compromise his client's interest if compelled to serve as an officer of the court rather

---

628. Rothwax, pp. 139,140
629. World, October 4, 2003, p. 25
630. World, October 4, 2003, p. 25
631. Journal, April 17, 1995, p. 34
632. Rothwax, p. 234

than as an advocate."[633] Apparently Professor Landsman prefers that the presiding judge sit on the bench as a dummy, a mere figurehead, one perhaps to preserve order but not to think or try to seek accuracy, and thus truth, in the proceedings. To do more, according to Professor Landsman, is to show partiality.

Judges should be worthier than that. And, if not, perhaps it is the fault of the manner in which the majority of our judges are chosen. Lawyers should not complain when they are part of those procedures. Most lawyers surely are intelligent, but as former prosecutor Bugliosi observes, "One thing I have seen over and over again in life is that there is virtually no correlation between intelligence and common sense." Common sense, of course, refers to good judgment.

No system will succeed if both of the opposing attorneys fail to serve as true officers of the court. A true officer of the court serves honorably and for the public good. It is doubtful that a zealous advocate of his or her client can serve honorably. John J. Curley, retired Chairman, President and CEO, Gannett Co. Inc., once said that "truth, fairness and integrity are hallmarks of great lawyers and judges"[634] Chief Justice E. Norman Veasey of the Delaware Supreme Court describes one way a great lawyer may retain his or her image. "When a client wants the 'meanest' lawyer available to aggressively take on the other side, the lawyer must just say 'no.'"[635]

Lawyer Katz was both pessimistic and optimistic when she wrote the following.

> In order to refresh the civil justice system, there are immediate tasks and there are long-term tasks. The immediate tasks involve correcting some of the more egregious dysfunctions and abuses. This must be primarily the work of judges, lawyers, and clients. For those attorneys—a small minority—who callously exploit and exacerbate the system's failures, an honest self-appraisal may be too much to expect. Some of these lawyers no doubt believe that this is how the world is supposed to work. As long as you don't explicitly and egregiously break the rules (or get caught breaking the rules), the clever

633. Landsman, p. 35
634. Journal, May 1994, p. 79
635. Journal, October, 1994 p. 104

are entitled to take advantage of the less clever. This type of lawyer won't get the message until it is in his or her personal interest to do so. But for the many lawyers who are unsettled by what they see and experience, yet who have no idea what to do about it, there are plenty of opportunities available.[636]

Reform will never be easy. Professor Friedman, quoting another source, said that "lawyers 'as a body never did begin a reform of the law, and, judging from experience, they never will.'"[637] Still, there is hope. Writer Olson, a non-lawyer incidentally, wrote that "within the American legal profession, probably a solid majority already would like to see the fighting deescalate. Even many lawyers who are doing well financially out of the strife would be happy to make a bit less money if a more rational and civilized style of practice could result."[638]

An article in the *ABA Journal* discusses the difficulty that adversarial lawyers have when representing clients who have a special problem such as drug dependency. These clients need medical help, but it is doubtful that attorneys defending them try to help them by, in effect, "turning them in." In this same Journal discussion, Exeter, New Hampshire lawyer Lawrence Vogelman, who is on the board of the National Association of Criminal Defense Lawyers, makes this odd statement. "The obligation of defense lawyers is to fight for their clients. Prosecutors and judges have the additional obligation to ensure justice is done, but defense lawyers must single-mindedly represent clients—the innocent as well as the guilty. 'People can't lose sight of the fact that the defense attorney is the only person in the room whose obligation is *not* to do justice.'"[639]

Those lawyers that worship the trial for one reason or another will always justify the trial. According to an *ABA Journal* eReport, "Case filings are up, and parties spend more money on pretrial work. Yet fewer actions actually go to trial—and all of this is troubling many litigators...If fewer cases get tried, less attorneys get actual

---

636. Katz, p. 154
637. Friedman(2), p. 404
638. Olson, p. 244
639. Journal, February 2003, p. 36

court experience...[and] there's a concern that...parties are not getting their day in court."[640] That statement is really quite degrading to the law profession.

Writer Olson also blames this trial stance upon "many of the professors who began to dominate elite law schools during [the 1960s and 1970s]."

> According to this new view, litigation deters wrongful conduct: The more lawsuits that are filed, the more people will behave carefully. Litigation also came to be seen as a way to redistribute wealth from those who have it to those who need it. From this perspective, the more litigation there is, the more redistributive justice the courts can impose on society. And who can be against justice?[641]

Lawyer Katz would not agree with that last statement concerning the redistribution of wealth, she writing that "clients and the general public must change their own ways. They need to stop thinking of lawsuits as potential windfalls or basic competitive tools."[642] Yet how can this attitude actually change when, according to lawyer Crier, "litigation is no longer a crapshoot, it is becoming a sure thing. If you can't get a satisfactory nuisance settlement, then try your case; the awards are phenomenal!"[643]

Somehow, it doesn't seem right to end this chapter on that note. As a group, lawyers are not villains. The good ones are far in the majority and many have passionately called for reform.[644] The bar, however, is apathetic as to the fact that an adversarial system of justice elevates winning over truth. Their passivity gives the impression to the general public that the law profession is less than admirable. The bar's lack of interest in truly reforming the judicial system is confounding, since it is the court system that sets the tone for the reputation of the profession, not what the bar claims it to be. (Author's note: He has been a member of the ABA since 1956 and a member of his local and state bars since long before that. As with

---

640. ABA Journal eReport, December 19, 2003, p .1
641. Imprimis, March 2004, p. 2
642. Katz, p. 146
643. Crier, p. 9
644. Katz, p. 144

most memberships, this does not signify that he agrees with everything that such organizations do or fail to do or say or don't say.)

THE PUBLIC'S PERCEPTION

Judge Neely stated that "every system of government is composed of two separate systems—a myth system, which is how people expect government to operate, and an operational system, which is how government actually operates."[645] Apply that statement to the US system of justice. No doubt, due to its constant promotion by trial attorneys, the general public believes that our judicial system is not only the best system but also the only system that arrives at truth. That is the myth.

The actuality is that "the process requires the prosecution to present its case in the most awkward way possible...the last thing a witness is allowed to do is tell his story in his own words and give his opinion of what it means."[646] As interminably stated, contrary to the public's expectations, the trial lawyers' goal is not to ascertain the truth but to win. That is not to say that the expectations and the perceptions are the same.

As Judge Rothwax observed, "We have never resolved the issue of the proper balance between zealous representation and the obligation of the lawyer to the court and to the public."[647] This would not be a problem if the *ABA Model Rules* did not emphasize, in fact require, "zealous" representation,[648] a guiding principle enthusiastically endorsed and faithfully followed by most trial lawyers. Somehow, "zealousness" and all its relations, such as fanaticism, connote a fight or bitter antagonism and that is what results in a courtroom brawl that entails such representation.

Lawyer Rosenberg remarked during the Simpson trial that "many people seem to view the justice system as a pristine search for

645. Neely, p. 18
646. Journal, January 1991, p. 60
647. Rothwax, p. 141
648. Rules, Preamble [2] and [9], pp. 1,2

truth, where lawyers on both sides ought to serve as assistant truth-seekers. Many people's comments appear to suggest that they would be more comfortable, at least in theory, with an inquisitorial system based on the European model."[649] Dean Pound said mostly the same thing one hundred years previously,[650] but to no avail. Bar leaders have a different perception than does the public. In 1989, ABA President Robert D. Raven, now Senior of Counsel in San Francisco, listed what he believed to be the major issues, but none of them touched upon the adversarial system.[651]

ABA Foundation researcher Tom Tyler, Professor of Psychology, New York University School of Law, discovered, surprisingly, that "people often care less about how much money they get than about the process by which they got it. 'Clients care most about the process by which their problem or dispute is resolved. In particular, people place great weight on having their problem or dispute settled in a way they feel is fair.'"[652] Although that observation was made in relation to civil cases, yet public polls indicate large numbers "express disgust...with lawyers generally, and, above all, with the criminal justice system as a whole."[653]

Lawyer Toothman observed that "the legal system will never be universally popular as long as it produces losers as well as winners."[654] This probably is due to the existing system, which induces parties to believe that they can "win" regardless of the strength of their case. This "win" syndrome creates a problem for the conscientious lawyer who may believe a potential case has no merit and thus may want to refuse it contrary to his or her client's wishes. However, Professor Landsman has a solution. "The situations in which the attorney must reject his client's wishes should be clearly and narrowly defined...otherwise a chill will be cast over the rela-

---

649. Journal, June 1995, p. 74
650. Pound, generally
651. Journal, April 1989, p. 8
652. Journal, July 1, 1988, p. 28
653. Journal, June 1995, p. 77
654. Journal, September 1995, p. 80

tionship and over the entire adversary process."[655] That should be reason enough to do away with the present process.

A comprehensive survey of the public revealed that only twenty-nine percent indicated the most important role of lawyers was to serve as "an advocate for clients." On the other hand, from a list of legal reform priorities, fifty-nine percent, by far the largest percentage, believed that lawyers' ethics should have top priority.[656] This tells us something about the system of justice. It is impossible for lawyers to be ethical when, first of all, they are expected to be a zealous advocate, because the two are incompatible.

---

655. Landsman, p. 29
656. Journal, September 1993, p. 64

CHAPTER 9. RECOMMENDATIONS

According to lawyer Katz, "there are now tremendous and damaging gaps between the contemporary legal system, which we call an adversary system, and that system as it should be. The present system is simply too adversarial."[657] Then she adds:

> There will be no meaningful reform until two powerful groups—lawyers and their clients—are ready to face up to the reality that our present system cannot provide dependable justice in the 20th century, let alone the 21st. Thus, the first step toward implementation of my (or any) serious proposal is to recognize just how badly the system has deteriorated...It is time to admit that we are on a very slippery slope. To expect more and more of a dangerously deteriorating system is folly. To regard litigation as a game is to strip it of the sense of justice. To impose exorbitant penalties unjustly is to subject to arbitrary and capricious tyranny.

> People know it. Clients know it. Many judges know it. Deep in their hearts, many lawyers know it...If my fellow lawyers, whom I hold in high regard, can shed that trinity of evasions—blind defense, cynical acceptance, and ineffectual self-criticism—the result will benefit the profession, the system, and the country.[658]

---

657. Katz, p. 75
658. Katz, pp. 143,144

The term "adversarial justice" properly describes America's judicial system, a court system that encourages, actually mandates, parties to contend against each other. When a conflict reaches the trial stage, if not before, the attorneys are expected to fight relentlessly on behalf of their respective clients with the goal of winning. Such a system degrades the legal profession, since rarely do both sides attempt to discover and reveal the entire truth. It is incomprehensible why our bar leaders tout, and our judiciary tolerate, such a system. If it is because of tradition, then that is a flimsy excuse for continuing a procedure harmful to society and that disgraces the legal profession as well as the judiciary. Former ABA President Robert J. Grey Jr. did suggest some substitute, but inconclusive, remedies when he wrote.

> A trial is not always the best way to resolve a dispute. Lawyers have to know when mediation, negotiation and arbitration—or more innovative methods like summary jury trial—are the best use of resources to achieve a just solution."[659]

Dean Pound's thinking in 1906 was so far ahead of his colleagues that he was but a voice in the wilderness, although lawyer Rembar believed that he led "the twentieth-century movement for reform."[660] Rembar's book, *The Law of the Land*, contains a subtitle, *The Evolution of our Legal System*, the latter of which is an accurate description of our snail pace of change. Perhaps Judge Neely explained why when he said that "court reform requires the active support of political institutions."[661]

Reform should have only one goal: to make those changes that will primarily lead to truth and accuracy in our judicial system. Any other issues, such as speed or cost of resolution, although important, will tend to sidetrack the main goal. The purpose of a court is to find the truth and to rule accordingly. Anything that obstructs this process should be jettisoned and anything that facilitates this process should be embraced.

---

659. Journal, July 2005, p. 6
660. Rembar, p. 249
661. Neely, p. 22

Lawyers should constantly remind themselves of the stated purpose of a trial, that is, to determine which party is wrong and which one is right. Otherwise, a trial is merely a farce or a gimmick engaged in to ostensibly settle a conflict.

Judge Rothwax did not state a mere rhetorical question when he questioned who would correct the system of justice, the lawyers or the judges. He said the latter. "Lawyers simply are not the appropriate persons to correct the defects of the adversarial system. Their hearts will never be in it, and it is unfair to both their clients and themselves to require them to serve two masters. We must take action on a judicial level to right the wrongs that neither side in the adversary system is capable of righting."[662]

Elliot Bien would seem to agree.[663] Judge Rothwax was probably correct, if what Professor Friedman says is true. "'Law reform,' in the sense the organized bar uses this term, is really a measure for professional defense. It responds mostly to the sense of beleaguered comradeship, which characterizes the elite of the profession...Law reform was one way of showing the world that lawyers too served the public interest; and law reform has been historically linked, since the 1870s, with the official organization of the bar."[664]

Judge Rothwax may not have it quite correct. Our government may well initiate reform of our legal system, not the judges, since it is doubtful that the legal profession or even the judiciary will initiate reform. In 2005, British Lord Charles Falconer, Secretary of State for Constitutional Affairs and Lord Chancellor, announced "a package of measures to make the regulatory and discipline process for lawyers more open and accountable to the public...[he stating that] 'Reform of legal services is overdue.'"[665]

Lawyer Kagan was not thinking in terms of abolishing the adversarial process, but merely in improving it, when he wrote the following. As you read it, however, consider how nice it would be if adversaryism itself were nonexistent.

---

662. Rothwax, p. 142
663. Judicature, November-December 2002, p. 132
664. Friedman(2), p. 674
665. www.abanet.org/journal/ereport/albrit.html

Adversarial legalism would almost surely decline if the federal and state constitutions were amended to abolish the privilege [against self-incrimination] whenever defendants in legal proceedings are granted strong *institutional* protections against coercion, abuse, harassment, or trickery. For example, criminal defendants (like other citizens who have relevant knowledge) could be legally obligated to testify at trial, as long as a competent defense lawyer is present to object to misleading or bullying questions.[666]

Professor Landsman mentions three professors who are concerned that too many settled cases, which would include plea-bargaining, could endanger the adversarial system. What they claim is that "a certain number of trials is needed to ensure the continuing credibility of the system. If the number of litigated cases shrinks too drastically, the continuing efficacy of the system may be called into question."[667] These professors could also have mentioned the ADRs, a term that stands for Alternative Dispute Resolution. ADRs primarily involve arbitration and mediation. It does not take any imagination to realize why ADRs have become so popular.

Writer Olson possibly indicates why. "As individuals and in our larger associations, we are most of us terribly vulnerable to the perils of litigation. Yet as a society, we are in no sense helpless to move against its evils. All it takes is the will. The will may not be here yet, but it is coming. When it does, we will again make litigation an exception, a last resort, a necessary evil at the margins of our common life."[668]

In an *ABA Journal* article, Olson elaborated. "The good news is that things don't have to be that way. The answer is to reform litigation, to make it less threatening to those caught up in it. That means revamping procedures and substantive laws in ways that will de-escalate the tactical arms race, limiting and resolving disputes rather than exacerbating them. It means putting a price tag on needless lawsuits by recognizing the right of wrongly sued persons to recover reasonable expenses from their adversaries."[669]

---

666. Kagan, p. 234
667. Landsman, p. 22
668. Olson, p. 348
669. Journal, October 1991, p. 71

Not all individuals or groups, of course, will agree to eliminate the adversarial system. One of these groups apparently is the AJS, which defines itself as follows. "The American Judicature Society is a nonpartisan organization with a national membership of judges, lawyers, and non-legally trained citizens interested in the administration of justice."[670] In an editorial entitled *Eavesdropping on the Adversary System*, the AJS criticized decisions taken by Attorney General Ashcroft relative to terrorism. Among the AJS's comments were the following.

> This remarkable departure from existing law holds the potential to violate the Sixth Amendment right to counsel and the Fourth Amendment right to privacy, and makes a shambles of the attorney-client privilege.... There are few principles more essential to the fair and effective administration of justice than protection of attorney-client communications that are intended to be confidential...it will chill—indeed, freeze—the ability of counsel and client to communicate privately and confidentially. The result will inevitably be an inability to render effective assistance of counsel.[671]

Although unusual for anyone to do so, quite correctly the AJS interrelated the attorney-client privilege with the US system. As the AJS understood, in contested matters, the absence of one means the end of the other. Thus those who worship the attorney-client privilege will fight the demise of this system. The reverse, of course, is also true. Yet consider the AJS's statement "to render effective assistance of counsel." It is difficult to comprehend what is meant by "effective" as it is used. The word "effective" connotes winning, which is not what trials should be about. Those statements, or similar ones, shame the legal profession.

Consider also its statement about the "fair and effective administration of justice." Apparently, the word "justice" as used here connotes that accused persons should possess the opportunity to avoid conviction even though in fact they are guilty. If so, this is another shameful position for the legal profession to take.

---

670. About AJS at Web site ajs.org/ajs/ajs_about. asp, p. 1
671. AJS at Web site ajs.org/ajs/ajs_editorial-template.asp?content_id=25 pp. 1,2

None of these comments are meant to ignore the Bill of Rights. It is only that it is a stretch to believe that these Rights were meant by our Makers to make it possible for the guilty to be found innocent. Surely, these Rights were only meant to make it difficult for the innocent to be found guilty. To believe otherwise would actually be doing an injustice to our Makers. As frequently stated, the goal should be truth, not winning. This will be difficult for those lawyers who have a temptation to tally their "wins."[672] As adversaryism attests, truth is difficult to attain when both parties do not have the same goal—that of finding the truth.

Many elements relate to the elimination of our adversarial system of justice. Mere elimination of the adversarial process and its bedmate, the attorney-client privilege, in matters of conflict will not of itself completely create a judicial system we can all be proud of. For a better, genuinely workable, and just system, other things need to be addressed as well. These are listed numerically below, more or less in the order of this book. Their order, however, does not signify the order of their importance, since all of them are important.

1. THE LEGAL PROFESSION.

The ABA must revise its *Model Rules of Professional Conduct*. Currently, trial lawyers have an obviously irreconcilable conflict between "zealous" advocacy and serving as "an officer of the legal system and a public citizen having special responsibility for the quality of justice."[673] The Rules mandate that the attorney "shall abide by the client's decision...as to a plea to be entered"[674] A comment then states that "lawyers usually defer to the client regarding...concern for third persons who might be adversely affected."[675] Another Rule confirms the sacrosanct principle that communications between attorney-client are secret. "A funda-

---

672. Journal, June 2004, p. 74
673. Rules, p. 1. See also, p. 15
674. Rules, p. 12
675. Rules, p. 13

mental principle in the client-lawyer relationship is that...the lawyer must not reveal information relating to the representation.... This contributes to the trust that is the hallmark of the client-lawyer relationship."[676]

It is obvious that little value, if any, is given by the Rules to lawyers serving as officers of the court. Doing away with the adversarial system of obtaining justice requires that all information concerning the dispute be voluntarily presented to and by both parties, and eventually to the court if the conflict reaches that point. It is of much greater importance and much more professional that lawyers act at the higher level of being officers of the court rather than at the lower level of zealously advocating for their clients regardless of their guilt or liability. Judge Gerber was apparently of the same mind when he recommended "Why not consider a new ethics rule making a lawyer's first loyalty not to the client but to the law?"[677]

The *ABA Model Rules* need to be redrafted to make it clear that the attorneys' first loyalties are to the court. They should truly be officers of the court, the Rules not just a sham. Lawyers should not be referred to as "advocates," somewhat a fighting term, but rather as representatives. Especially should the word "zealous," another fighting term, be eliminated from the Rules.

The Rules need to be changed to clearly state that the confidences and secrets of a client apply only to uncontested matters. The Rules must clearly state that the US judicial system is inquisitorial, not adversarial, and that it is the duty and obligation of lawyers to seek and speak nothing but the truth. Think how prestigious that would be for lawyers. What an admirable change this would make in their reputation. More importantly, think how notably remarkable and healthy that would be for society.

Adversaryism and client confidentiality go hand in hand. One cannot be eliminated without the other. Bear in mind that client confidences are validly important and should be perpetually maintained in private matters between lawyer and client, but *only* if no

---

676. Rules, p. 22
677. Journal, January 1993, p. 112

conflict or contest exists as to a third party. However, if a matter is in dispute, then all the information and facts should be on the table, fully transparent, even though one or both parties are adversely affected by such openness. Lawsuits are not a game to be won by the best finagler. What each lawyer knows or should know should not be withheld from the other. Secrets are what create the adversarial atmosphere. Truth withheld engenders conflict. Trial lawyers know that, although not all of them, to their credit, use that to their advantage.

Judge Rothwax would take it another step. "What would be so wrong with a system that requested a defendant to testify in a court of law, on the record, and in the presence of his lawyers and the judge, after a showing of his probable guilt had been demonstrated by the evidence?"[678] And, he continues, if the defendant does not, why can't the judge instruct the jury "that they might draw an adverse inference from his failure to deny or explain the evidence against him?"[679] Of course, our Supreme Court would have to think this out a bit more carefully and change their tune accordingly.

Professor Landsman perhaps reveals why some lawyers resist the termination of this process. "Lawyers play a far less important role [under the European system] than they do in the adversary system."[680] In other words, American trial lawyers may be afraid of losing their prominence in the courtroom if the adversarial system disappeared. In writing that, however, Professor Landsman was under the impression that the alternative to our present system was the European system, which imposes upon the presiding judge the responsibility of eliciting information from the witnesses. By no means is the European system the only alternative, although that is the popular belief, a belief that may be promulgated by those who want to retain our present system. In an inquisitorial system, absolutely no reason exists why two honest lawyers cannot elicit the truth, the same as one honest judge.

---

678. Rothwax, p. 231
679. Rothwax, p. 231
680. Landsman, p. 38

Other reasons exist why trial lawyers should abandon the adversarial process. A recent article in the *ABA Journal*[681] discusses using "a hands-on approach to solving problems rather than simply winning cases," something described as "putting therapeutic jurisprudence to work." While dissolution of marriage cases is mentioned, other types of cases, even tort cases, are also suggested. Quite obviously, doing away with the adversarial process would make therapeutic goals more realistic and put lawyers in a better light.

Many lawyers, presumably even some trial lawyers, are not happy in their profession. Some have turned to mediation as an alternative;[682] others have resorted to alcohol or drugs, something the bar does not openly discuss. Judge Horn quotes a source that says this.

> Report after report tells us that lawyers experience psychological unrest at much higher levels than non-lawyers. A survey of 105 occupations showed lawyers first on the list in experiencing depression; another study reports that fully *one-third* of all attorneys suffer from either depression, alcohol or drug abuse...anxiety and obsessive behavior afflict a disproportionately large number of lawyers, sometimes to the point of incapacitation; many lawyers report strong feeling of isolation and social alienation; and upwards of sixty percent of lawyers say they would not recommend the law as a career to their own children.[683]

It seems that the way law is practiced in contested matters is the primary reason. Students entering law schools are often idealistic. Their ideals surely are shattered before they even graduate.

A growing number of lawyers have begun bypassing the adversarial system in civil cases under a process called "collaborative law." This is what Steven Keeva says, in part, about this relatively new development.

> In collaborative law, parties come together for the sole purpose of resolving disputes—out of court and with all information shared among lawyers and clients. What makes this possible is the fact that

---

681. Journal, May 2003, p. 54
682. Journal, June 2003, p. 66
683. Horn, p. 24

collaborative law practitioners forswear litigation and sign agreements to that effect. If the case cannot be settled and the clients decide they want to litigate, they have to find other lawyers to represent them. This setup creates such a strong incentive to reach agreement that the collaborative process is overwhelmingly effective. People [meaning lawyers] often come to collaborative law out of despair... They were drawn to law...because they saw potential for healing. Instead, they found carnage.... They become mediators. But collaborative law offers something that mediation doesn't: It lets you continue to practice law, that is to be an advocate rather than a neutral, and to offer legal advice.... "We're not here to fight."...For many people it's a last gasp before leaving the practice, and suddenly they see an opportunity for doing healing work.[684]

Jill Schachner Chanen wrote a long article in the *ABA Journal* entitled "Collaborative Counselors." In part, this is what she said:

[Collaborative practice lawyers] believe this newest entry into the alternative dispute resolution scene may be just the tool that clients are seeking to help them navigate a civil justice system that increasingly relies on expensive tactics that work against their interests...Some observers say the practice, which promotes clients' free exchange of information in settlement negotiations by barring its use in court, could be a ready alternative both to litigation and mediation in a variety of civil practice areas...The idea of collaborative law was the brainchild of one man—Minneapolis lawyer Stu Webb—who wasn't satisfied with the litigation-based model of family law practice. [Webb devised] collaborative law, where the rules and game-playing associated with litigation are discarded in favor of interest-based negotiation, with the clients fully and freely participating...Questions linger about the ethics of collaborative practice. Because of its unique format, many say it is impossible for lawyers to be zealous advocates for their clients.[685]

It is interesting—actually mystifying—to note that dissenters to the system cite "ethics" as a reason for discontinuing its use. Regardless, lawyers engaged in collaborative law are sending out a warning to the rest of the profession. "Get your house in order or suffer the consequences."[686]

---

684. Journal, June 2003, pp. 66,67
685. Journal, June 2006, p. 52
686. The following Web sites offer more information about collaborative law: divorcenet.com/ca/tesler.html; collaborativedivorce.com; collabgroup.com

Various sovereignties are also sending out a message according to Sherman L. Cohn, Professor of Law, Georgetown Law Center in Washington, DC.

> [There is a] perceived failure of the profession to regulate itself in the public interest, requiring government to step in to do the job in which the profession failed...the concept of "public service" includes the representation of and loyalty to a client. But just as true are the limits on that "loyalty.".....if we, the legal profession, do not act as a profession—in Dean Pound's words, "in the spirit of a public ser-vice"—political branches of government will do it for us...if we wish to preserve our profession, we must realize that ethically we cannot take "loyalty" to a client to the limits of where the client would like to go...We must retain that independence from the client so that we can truly act "in the spirit of a public service." If we do not, the handwrit-ing is clear: others will do it for us, and our legitimate loyalty to client will ultimately be washed away.[687]

As mentioned earlier, an evolution in the judicial process is slowly becoming apparent. The word "evolution" refers to a gradual change. In this instance, it means a slow, actually a very slow, change in lawyer-client relationships and the judicial process. Trial lawyers, especially criminal defense lawyers, are not yet hanging on by their fingernails, however. Real change for the better can only occur by a revolution, not evolution, in such relationships and process in order that real reform can occur. This means that bar leaders and the judiciary must show true leadership to fully reform the system of justice in all its aspects. Law professors, especially those teaching ethics and trial practice, must also be part of this process.

Some hope once seemed to be on the horizon. Mostly because of the Enron and similar situations, the ABA formed a Task Force on Corporate Responsibility. On March 31, 2003, the committee filed its report.[688] Inter alia, it suggested some loosening up, but not much, of the sacrosanct lawyer-client relationship. The report rec-ommended that lawyers be allowed—not mandated—to tattle on

---

687. Lawyer, May 2003, pp. 17,18
688. The full report is available on the ABA's web site, abanet.org. See also, Journal, July 2003, p. 8.

their clients under certain circumstances.[689] Referring to the report, then ABA President Alfred P. Carlton Jr. stated that "this report will be a desktop reference for years to come for lawyers who seek to honor their profession's core commitment to clients while maintaining their professional responsibility to be officers of the court."[690] It is somewhat disheartening, since it appears that that was as far as the ABA would go. As long as client secrecy is allowed to exist in a contested setting, reform of the adversarial process will languish.

Worse, it appears that the ABA has about-faced. An *ABA Journal* article stated that "lawyers representing corporations have expressed concern that the legal protections afforded by the attorney-client privilege and work-product doctrine are eroding."[691] Perhaps in response to those concerns, another Task Force created in September 2004 by then ABA President Robert J. Grey Jr. issued the following statement. "It is important for the ABA to affirm bedrock principles [referring to the attorney-client privilege and the work-product doctrine] that will be the foundation for its further work."[692]

In spite of some movement in the courts to the contrary notwithstanding,[693] the same *Journal* article further reported as follows.

> It is widely recognized that the attorney-client privilege protects confidential communications between lawyer and client, while the work-product doctrine provides qualified protection to writings embodying an attorney's factual investigations, research, impressions, opinions and conclusions in anticipation of litigation. The attorney-client privilege encourages clients to make disclosures necessary to obtain legal assistance, while the work-product doctrine allows lawyers to investigate, prepare and develop strategy relating to litigation without worrying about adversaries obtaining their work and using it against their clients.

---

689. See p. 52 of the report.
690. Journal, July 2003, p. 8
691. Journal, December 2005, p. 62
692. Journal, December 2005, p. 61
693. See the ABA Journal article of December 2005, pp. 61-65

Both the attorney-client privilege and the work-product doctrine restrict a third party's use of legal compulsion, such as a court order backed by the threat of a contempt sanction to obtain protected information. While potentially impeding third-party access to relevant evidence, the privilege and doctrine are understood to serve a paramount public interest: The public benefits when parties obtain effective assistance from lawyers who advise them how to act in conformity with the complexities of the law, or who present legitimate claims of defenses on their behalf in litigation.[694]

Bruce A. Green, Louis Stein Professor of Law at Fordham University School of Law in New York City and David C. Clifton, an associate at McKenna Lone & Aldridge in Atlanta wrote the *Journal* article. Green is the reporter and Clifton is an associate reporter for the ABA Task Force on the Attorney-Client Privilege. A reading of that quote indicates that the ABA intends to resist any attempt to nullify even a part of the attorney-client privilege, regardless of the negative effect it has on the reputation of both the judicial system and the legal profession.

Indeed, resistance to a change in the attorney-client privilege continues vigorously by the ABA. All of the following information concerning this topic, through the February 2006 communication below, was obtained from two ABA websites[695] and their various links.

On July 13, 2005, the Executive Council of the Association of Defense Trial Attorneys approved a Resolution that endorsed the ABA's position on the attorney-client privilege. It was not until August 9, 2005, however, that the ABA House of Delegates actually adopted the twenty-five page Report of The Task Force on the Attorney-Client Privilege. Former ABA President R. William Ide III as Chair signed this Report on May 18, 2005. Part of the Report, which will be commented on later, stated as follows.

The confidentiality of the attorney-client relationship has historically been considered an essential aspect of legal representation, and one that is necessary to ensure the ability of lawyers to carry out their

---

694. Journal, December 2005, pp. 61,62
695.   http://abanet.org/media/youraba/200602/article05.html, and http://www.abanet.org/buslaw/attorneyclient/

assigned role in the legal system. The confidential relationship is recognized and preserved not only in the common law regulating the lawyer-client relationship and in the rules of professional conduct, but in the attorney-client privilege and, with respect to the lawyer's role in litigation, the work-product doctrine.

The attorney-client privilege is a rule of evidence that protects the confidentiality of communications between an attorney and client. Its underlying purpose is to encourage persons to seek legal advice freely and to communicate candidly during consultations with their attorneys without fear that the information will be revealed to others. This enables clients to receive the most competent legal advice from fully informed counsel so that the client can fulfill his or her responsibilities under the law and benefit from the law's protection. Given the ever-growing and increasingly complex body of public law, the client's better understanding of his or her legal obligations enhances the law's efficacy.

Recognizing that the attorney-client privilege is an exception—albeit a very important exception—to the general principle that witnesses must provide relevant testimony in court proceedings, courts over the decades have sought to develop the parameters of the privilege toward several ends. Importantly, the privilege has been designed to apply only in the general class of cases where its purposes are strongly served. In general, attorney-client communications will only be privileged if the communication was between a lawyer and a client (or prospective client), was for the purpose of enabling the client to secure legal services or assistance (and not for the purpose of committing a crime), and was made in confidence (i.e., outside the presence of third parties). Thus, the mere fact that an individual communicates with an attorney does not make the communication privileged. Personal communications, business advice, and advice to aid in the commission of illegal activity that is carried out are not protected. The client claiming the benefit of the privilege has the burden of proving its applicability, and the privilege is lost if the client does not claim the privilege or waives it.

The attorney-client privilege is subject to limited exceptions, but importantly, it is *not* subject to an exception simply because a private litigant, government agency, or other third party claims an important need to know what the client discussed with an attorney. Such an exception has been rejected primarily because of the paramount importance of assuring clients in advance whether their communications will be privileged. If the protection were not assured, the client would be unable to rely on confidentiality when seeking legal advice, and hence might be hesitant to disclose adverse as well as favorable facts to the lawyer. Further, it is crucial to remember that the privilege does not shut off access to facts within a party's possession. A party can be asked, "what did you observe?" or "what did you do?" The only type of question that the privilege forecloses, is, "What was your conversation with your lawyer?"

Critics of the privilege argue that because the privilege prevents the disclosure of a client's communications, it hinders the public's ability to discover the truth. This argument fails to account for the countervailing benefits associated with the privilege. As one writer has stated, '[T]he definition of the privilege [expresses] a value choice between protection of privacy and discovery of truth and the choice of either involves the acceptance of an evil—betrayal of confidence or suppression of truth.' The judiciary has recognized this choice and has consistently decided in favor of upholding and protecting the privilege.

The work-product doctrine is a protection afforded to the 'work product' of attorneys that precludes adversaries from discovering 'work product' developed in anticipation of litigation...the privilege belongs only to the client.

While the privilege and the work-product doctrine will often overlap in their protection, they are by no means coextensive. The work-product doctrine offers a broader protection than the privilege in that it can encompass not only communications, but also an attorney's thoughts, impressions, beliefs and materials. Despite being broader than the privilege in that respect, the work-product doctrine is only applicable to 'work product' prepared in anticipation of litigation.[696]

On November 15, 2005, Donald C. Klawiter, Chair of the ABA Antitrust Law Section of the ABA, presented a statement before the United States Sentencing Commission, in which the attorney-client privilege was strongly endorsed. The following excerpt from the Task Force Mission Statement explains why the ABA is concerned about possible changes in the federal sentencing guidelines.

Among recent actions of the federal government affecting the [attorney-client] privilege that the Task Force should consider are the US Sentencing Commission's proposed amendments to the federal sentencing guidelines for corporations and other entities. These amendments include as a new factor in determining whether the entity has fully cooperated, and hence is entitled to leniency, whether the entity and its employees waive attorney-client privilege and work product protections. In addition, the US Justice Department and the

---

696. http://www.abanet.org/buslaw/attorneyclient/ July 28, 2006, pp. 2,3,4

Securities and Exchange Commission, as well as other federal agencies, have also recently adopted policies requiring waiver of the privilege as a condition for cooperation. Moreover, while some federal agencies have entered into confidentiality agreements with the parties providing the agencies with privileged information, their effectiveness in protecting that information from further disclosure is in doubt.

Examining the reporting on these and related issues will enable the American Bar Association and its Task Force to educate policy makers and the public on the importance of maintaining the attorney-client privilege against unreasonable governmental efforts to circumvent its effectiveness.[697]

On January 23, 2006, the *New Jersey Law Journal* presented an editorial in which it was stated that the "attorney-client and work-product protections are under attack. These protections are essential to the adversary process and crucial to attorneys as counselors and advocates. Recent US Department of Justice policies and the US Sentencing Guidelines have begun to erode these protections in federal criminal investigations and prosecutions. We must defend these vital protections against such encroachment."[698]

This same editorial stated that it was joining the ABA, the American College of Trial Lawyers, the US Chamber of Commerce, and the Association of Corporate Counsel, all of whom oppose "measures and policies that effectively force waiver of these vital protections." The letter of January 31 immediately mentioned below states that the American Civil Liberties Union is also among the groups objecting to the new guidelines. These are strange bedfellows, except that each organization must feel that they have special interests that need defending, rather an indefensible and selfish position. The right to thwart the law with the adversarial process and the attorney-client privilege is still paramount in some circles. They are shaming their members by making it appear that they need this protection.

On January 31, 2006, ABA President Michael S. Greco addressed a letter to state and local bar leaders urging "help and

---

697. http://www.abanet.org/buslaw/attorneyclient/ July 28, 2006, p. 2
698. 183 N.J.L.J.214, January 23, 2006

support in preserving the attorney-client privilege and work product doctrine." On February 28, 2006, an email from the ABA went out to members of the ABA summarizing the ABA efforts relative to the attorney-client privilege and the work product doctrine and again urging their support. Finally, on June 29, 2006, an email from the ABA went out to the members, in which it was stated that the "ABA urges Attorney General to modify attorney-client privilege waiver policy. The ABA is encouraging the Justice Department to stop the increasingly common practice of federal prosecutors requiring organizations to waive their attorney-client privilege and work product protections as a condition for receiving 'cooperation credit' during investigations."

This last email links to http://www.abanet.org/media/youraba/200606/article03.html, which refers to a May 2 letter written by ABA President Michael Greco to Attorney General Alberto Gonzales. This letter states, in part, the following:

> As you know, the attorney-client privilege enables both individual and organizational clients to communicate with their lawyers in confidence, and it encourages clients to seek out and obtain guidance in how to conform their conduct to the law.

Unfortunately, it does seem that these various organizations, when seeking reform or protecting the status quo, whichever suits them best, do have merely their own special interests in mind. An example: The Institute for Legal Reform is a stated affiliate of the US Chamber of Commerce mentioned above. According to its website, the Institute (ILR) "is a national campaign, representing the nation's business community, with the critical mission of making America's legal system simpler, fairer and faster for everyone...[it is] the only national legal reform advocate to approach reform comprehensively, not only through changing the laws, but also by changing the legal culture and the legislators and judges that create that culture."[699]

However, in spite of their broadly stated agenda, it would appear from that website and its various links that their primary

---

699. http:/www.instituteforlegalreform.org/about/

concern is class action lawsuits. Nothing was found that indicated any concern for America's court system, a change of which probably would resolve much of their distress.

Interestingly, a full-page ad by the ILR in *USA Today* on March 29, 2006, did not mention class actions, but it did state that "lawsuit abuse is a serious problem...demand that your elected officials fix the flaws in the justice system."[700] A noble assertion that somehow does not ring true.

It is difficult to understand why all this concern by the ABA and related groups as to the loss or erosion of the attorney-client privilege and work product doctrine. It seems more important to be more concerned, for example, about corporate responsibility and fair sentencing of criminals.

The reader should again review the Task Force Report provisions quoted above. Truth in a conflict is barely mentioned and not in a favorable light. From a lawyer's viewpoint, clients' interests should be of less importance than the reputation of lawyers. Secrets of one party should be of no more importance than the welfare of the opposing party or of society in general. Protecting clients from what they justly deserve is not a valid reason for secrecy. It is lamentable that lawyers' ethics are never a part of this discussion. The attorney's hiding of facts from the court should always be considered unethical and a cause for sanctions.

2. LEGAL PROCEDURES.

According to Professor Landsman, "The procedural and evidentiary rules governing the adversarial process have...been the target of reformers."[701] This is not surprising. The sacrosanct adversarial system frustrates those who seek a change to make truth paramount. Hence, reformers chip away at the fringes, doing the best they can to lessen the impact of a system that does not make truth

---

700. *USA Today*, March 29, 2006, p. 7A
701. Landsman, p. 23

its primary target. Under our system, truth is not the bull's-eye aimed for by at least one of the trial participants. Our adversarial system is just the opposite of the inquisitorial process, which "is firmly committed to the search for material truth."[702]

One of these chips on the fringes is the use of discovery procedures "in which lawyers force opponents to cough up information."[703] These generally take the form of what is called interrogatories, a practice under the rules of procedure whereby one party poses a set of written questions to the other party. Another form of discovery is the deposition, a procedure whereby a layperson is deposed, that is, questioned, under oath. Oftentimes, these procedures are not much more than what writer Olson, among others, calls a "fishing expedition,"[704] in which the plaintiff is trying to discover something to sue about, this after he or she has already instigated suit. When discovery is mandated or made automatic by court rules, "it's a radical departure from the adversary system."[705]

The exclusionary rules, which exclude presentment of evidence that was obtained in a manner deemed unlawful by the courts, have nothing to do with the guilt or innocence of the accused. Examples of such alleged illegal conduct are unlawful search and seizure, no prior warning of the right to remain silent (Miranda Rule), and unlawful detention.[706] On the face of it, these rights must be maintained, but appellate courts are unable to make a distinction "whether a particular violation was intentional or merely negligent."[707] Total victory for those who champion truth rather than procedure would be to subject the violators to sanction rather than to allow the accused to go free because of some exclusionary rule. Judge Rothwax reacts to some of the exclusionary rules in this way.

---

702. Landsman, p. 38
703. Olson, p. 98
704. Olson, p. 114
705. Journal, April 1995, p. 20
706. Neely, p. 147
707. Neely, p. 147

The vast and unknowable search-and-seizure laws, based loosely on the Fourth Amendment, must be simplified and clarified to prevent a guessing game on the street and in the courtroom. As long as the law remains unknowable, there is no justification for the mandatory exclusionary rule. The Miranda ruling is an unnecessary overreaction to past abuses that videotapes and other technology can now preclude, and it should be abandoned...The right to an attorney should not be a factor in the investigative state, but only in the pretrial and trial stages. Asking questions and receiving answers from a suspect is a legitimate aspect of crime-solving.[708]

Not many commentators on the adversarial system take time to consider the hearsay rule, although writer Olson had some thoughts on the subject. "Letting in hearsay, opinion, and not-very-relevant evidence would cut down on the need for laborious circumlocution in leading courts toward desired factual conclusions. Admitting more grounds to balance in controversies and more guesswork as to what actually happened would let courts bypass technicalities and head straight for their intended result."[709] Absence of the adversarial process would almost entirely eliminate the hearsay rule and all of its numerous exceptions. In such a concordant setting, opposing counsel would be able to assess the value and truth of such proposed testimony.

3. THE JUDICIARY.

Theories abound as to what role presiding judges should assume.[710] These theories are mostly fenced in by the adversarial system, which restrains the judges' expertise and conduct. Whatever the system, trial judges should manage and conduct the trial. As presiding officers of the court, they must be active. If they are passive, both the trial and pretrial procedures suffer. But playing this role is quite difficult for judges in the milieu of the adversarial system. Fractious lawyers want no interference. It jeopardizes their

---

708. Rothwax, p. 237
709. Olson, p. 226
710. Landsman, pp. 77 etc.

case as they want it presented. When judges are active, truth is not in jeopardy, but the trial lawyer's case might be.

Possibly one of the reasons for the unspoken restraints put on state judges is that they are not totally trusted, at least in those thirty-nine states in which they are elected.[711] Merit selection and merit retention of these judges would add to the confidence of any judicial system, whether or not adversarial. Possibly nothing will change, but on July 11, 2000, the ABA House of Delegates did unanimously adopt a report setting standards "for judicial selection sometimes referred to as 'merit selection'."[712] In addition, the ABA Commission on the 21st Century Judiciary has made several recommendations, such as that "judges have retention elections rather than contested ones."[713]

In most federal district courts, "judges ask all the jury selection questions themselves in civil cases." Why? Because "most lawyers abuse the process by trying to sell their case instead of asking questions that will help select a jury."[714] This judicial activity would not be as necessary, although more acceptable to the attorneys, in a non-adversarial setting. Active judges can also do other things. They could explain to the jury different aspects of the trial as they occurred. In the adversarial setting, trial attorneys would froth at the mouth if judges did this, as trial attorneys want to run their own show. Judges could give the jury tentative instructions at the beginning of a trial so that the jury would know what to look for and consider as the trial proceeded. In the non-adversarial setting, the attorneys would welcome this. Judges could also better control and sanction the attorneys, but this would unlikely be as necessary in a non-adversarial system.

Perjury is prevalent in our courts,[715] but rarely noted and punished. No doubt this is due to our adversarial system. Judges would

---

711. Journal, May 2003, p. 20. See also, Journal, August 2003, p. 64
712. See ABA Web site, abanet.org, *Report of the Commission on State Judicial Selection Standards*, p. iv
713. Journal, August 2003, p. 64
714. Journal, July 2002, p. 55
715. Journal, May 1995, pp. 68, etc.

be more likely to take notice and intervene in a non-adversarial setting. Alternatively, this would not likely even be necessary if both attorneys were seeking the same goal, that of truth.

Lawyer Spence wrote that appellate judges should adopt the "conference method of...review."[716] The attorneys and the judge or judges would sit around a conference table and discuss the case. This type of trial was suggested as far back as 1980, whereby, "several witnesses to the same events testify concurrently."[717] Where no jury was involved, this could easily be accomplished by the judge, attorneys and called witness or witnesses all sitting around a counsel table. A little more imaginative seating and court structure would be involved if it were a jury trial. Adversarial attorneys would not like this scenario, but all the more reason for eliminating the system.

4. THE JURIES.

According to former ABA President Robert J. Grey, Jr., the jury "is one of the most important democratic institutions ever conceived and is still the bedrock of the justice system."[718] Firmly believing that, as previously mentioned, Grey made the strengthening of the jury system his primary objective during his term of office. In August 2004, he "launched the American Jury Initiative...In a two-pronged approach, Grey established the Commission on the American Jury...and the American Jury Project.... As a result, the ABA Principles for Juries and Jury Trials were adopted as policy by the House of Delegates in February 2005."[719]

The Principles constitute a twenty-five page report that show much welcome movement toward reform of America's jury system, such as the following (pp. 7 and 8 thereof): "Throughout the course of the trial, the court should provide instructions to the jury...

716. Spence, p. 267
717. Journal, August 1980, p. 967
718. Journal, April 2005, p. 61
719. Journal, April 2006, p. 71

[allow] note-taking and questioning by jurors...[inform the jurors of] the issues to be addressed, and the basic relevant legal principles, including the elements of the charges and claims and definitions...[and allow the jurors to discuss] the evidence among themselves...(p. 20) Parties and courts should be open to a variety of trial techniques to enhance juror comprehension of the issues."[720] Many of these recommendations were part of the "Standards Relating to Juror Use and Management," which had been previously adopted by the Judicial Division of the ABA.[721] The recommendations, acting as a catalyst, may result in a beneficial change from the customary jury passiveness.

As will be noted subsequently, many of these recommendations have already been in use in a limited number of courts. However, under our system of justice, it is doubtful that many trial lawyers, always having the goal of winning, would favor these changes. They might feel that such changes could endanger their presentation and thus would encroach upon their rights under our present system.

Absent the adversarial process, juries could be less common. This is not all bad, as long as the right to a jury trial remains absolute, available, and hindrance-free. As 2003-2004 Iowa Bar Association President Kevin Collins wrote, "As lawyers, we have a responsibility to work for the preservation of the jury system."[722] When a jury is chosen, however, everything should be done to help the jury make the right decision.[723] Obviously, though, under our present adversarial system, one of the opposing attorneys will not be keen about the jury arriving at the correct decision.

Because of their number, their lack of trial experience, and possibly because of their incompetence, juries cannot be as active as the presiding judge, but they can be more active then they generally are. Every juror should be given a pad and a pencil. They cannot be required to take notes, but the judge should encourage them to do

720. http://www.abanet.org/juryprojectstandards/home.html
721. http://www.abanet.org/jd/jurystandards/
722. Lawyer, November 2003, p. 5
723. See, e.g., Journal, August 7, 1989, p. 51

so. And, at the end of the testimony of each witness, the judge should ask the jurors if they have any questions. The American Jury Project agrees.[724]

As reported by the Associated Press, "Most states give judges the authority to allow jurors to ask questions. The practice is prohibited in Georgia, Minnesota, Mississippi, Nebraska and Texas, but has been upheld by every federal appeals court that has considered it, according to the National Center for State Courts."[725] However, this practice is not deemed common and is unpopular with at least some public defenders.[726]

But jurors, for their own peace of mind, should work for their measly pay. It should keep them more alert than they normally are. Especially should this jury activism be encouraged in our adversarial system, although this activity might fill up our mental institutions with trial attorneys. Yet, this might be one way to make the adversarial system more palatable. In a non-adversarial setting, no attorney, presumably always seeking the truth, would be fearful of such jury activity.

The American Judicature Society, in an editorial entitled *Jury Improvement, not Reform*, has this to say about juries.

> Among serious students of jury deliberations, there are many who would argue that the term 'jury reform' is a misnomer. As G. Thomas Munsterman of the National Center for State Courts has argued, a more appropriate term is 'jury improvement.' The jury improvement movement has included those who advocate more careful jury summoning and selection procedures; those who advocate streamlining trials to minimize the demands of jury service on citizens; those who advocate new procedures such as juror question asking and note taking during trials; and those who advocate allowing more frequent and clear communications between jury and judge or providing greater guidance to deliberating jurors.[727]

Under one of the American Bar Foundation's current research projects, "senior fellow Shari S. Diamond, also a law professor at

---

724. Journal, January 2005, p. 8
725. Gazette, May 1, 2005, p. 6A
726. ABA Journal eReport, May 13, 2005, p. 1
727. AJS at Web site ajs.org/ajs/ajs_editorial-template.asp?content_id=18, p. 1

Northwestern University in Chicago, is studying the effect of allowing jurors to discuss evidence throughout a trial."[728] This discussion among and between the jurors seems most logical, but under the US system, judges will often admonish the jurors not to talk about the case until after all the evidence has been presented. Trial attorneys themselves are not keen about jurors contemplating during the course of the trial. They want the jurors to keep a blank mind until the end of the trial at which time they will try to sway the jury to their point of view, regardless of what is right or just. It is no wonder that the legal profession suffers a poor reputation.

---

728. Journal, December 2005, p. 71

Conclusion

Lawyer Katz begins her book, *Justice Matters*, much the same as this book ends.

> As citizens, concerned about the integrity of the system, we know that something is wrong. We're worried. We ought to be. In fact, we should be appalled by the growing popular opinion that justice is no longer being served in the courts...Loss of respect for what happens in the court system ultimately means loss of respect for the law, and loss of respect for the law can be fatal to a democracy...As a lawyer, I'm concerned for my profession...I have no wish to harm my fellow lawyers...But I am persuaded that if the legal profession ignores the problem [of adversaryism] or, even worse, pretends that nothing is amiss, ultimately both the profession and the people will suffer.[729]

America's adversarial system of justice needs to be totally eliminated (even more so than Katz promotes) so that the judicial process does not shame both lawyers and judges, in fact the whole court system. This can be accomplished only by jettisoning the attorney-client privilege of confidentiality in contested situations, in other words, wherever and whenever conflict exists. Lawyers must be instilled with the idea that establishing the truth is more important than winning, a word that disgraces the legal profession and, in fact, our whole judicial system. Arthur E. Gamble, Chief

---

729. Katz, pp. 16,17,20

Judge, Iowa Judicial District 5C, touched upon this when he recently wrote that "lawyers cannot be excused for false statements on the basis of a sloppy, or even casual, unawareness of the truth. The administration of justice entrusted to our branch of government can be rendered only when our officers can be counted upon for absolute reliability and an impeccable reputation for honesty."[730]

One of the difficulties with reforming the judicial system is that the public has pigeonholed lawyers not as truth seekers but as connivers, a perception not far from the truth in many cases, particularly in criminal cases. Consider debate coaches. They teach their students to be able to take either side of an issue and when their students succeed, they are told that they would make good lawyers. In other words, to be a good lawyer, being truthful is not a concern; it is not even a factor. Being able to take a side and pretending it to be the truth is what counts.

By seeking truth, and being truthful in all things, the law profession will then actually earn a prominent place in society.

---

730. Lawyer, July 2003, p. 11

AUTHOR'S NOTE

This book has been written for everyone who is concerned about our adversarial judicial system, but it should be a mandatory read in Ethics 101 of every law school. Why? Because it points out the unethical flaws in our judicial system and how they can be remedied. One of these faults is the requirement that the trial attorney endure, to the exclusion of others, the secrets of the client. The result is that truth is often avoided or twisted, this in spite of what the trial attorney knows or should know or even wants to know. Dishearteningly, this occurs even though the trial attorney is characterized as an officer of the court, a misnomer of great significance.

Willing or not, the trial attorney in some respects has no choice. Mainly this is due to the *ABA Model Rules of Professional Conduct* and those states' canons of ethics that mirror such rules, rules that require both the attorney's zealous representation and the keeping of the attorney-client privilege of communication. Both, particularly the latter, are traditional and sacrosanct. Regardless, no rule, no matter how ancient or worshiped, should exist that mocks the US system of justice.

This privilege breeds adversaryiness, which the Model Rules describe as zealousness. The adversarial US system of justice is usually compared to the French inquisitorial system of justice, a contrast that may or may not be strictly correct since grades of each may overlap. Although perhaps merely a philosophical question, elimination of the US system of justice does not necessarily mean that any new system would be purely inquisitorial.

This author finds no fault with zealousness, except when it is utilized to distort or hide the truth. All persons involved in a suit, civil or criminal, are entitled to dedicated representation in order to avoid, for example, conviction of the innocent. But no attorney conduct should be condoned nor Rules utilized to avoid or evade the truth. Lawyers that participate in such irresponsible behavior should be sanctioned by the courts, since American citizens need to have total confidence in their judicial system, as well as in the legal profession. Such confidences are obviously lacking today.

This note is perhaps especially written to make certain that readers understand that in any contact between clients and their attorneys, other than in matters of conflict, what is said or revealed as between attorney and client is no one else's business. Except as noted, what the client discloses should be held in strict confidence as to third parties, unless the client agrees otherwise. These more common occurrences are private and need not be disclosed.

But suppose an attorney-client relationship concerns a third party conflict, or develops into one. When a contest arises or exists, whether or not foreseen, both parties as well as their attorneys should be required to make full disclosure. If clients lie or keep secrets to avoid liability or guilt, their attorneys should not mimic their clients. If they do, then in reality they are lowering themselves to the level of their clients, a level that some lawyers now seem to be satisfied with.

The law profession has suffered an unfavorable reputation seemingly from time immemorial. This reputation is justified in many instances. How could it be otherwise when the combination of the adversarial system and the attorney-client privilege of communication puts lawyers in a bad light and makes them suspect. Surely, this historical position has long given the public the impression, probably correctly, that lawyers are no better than their clients. This situation is not surprising when lawyers are trained and expected to win regardless of the circumstances.

The law profession has long been described as one of the true professions. Among other things, this connotes that lawyers, like other age-old professions, have higher standards than the general public. Actually, many other classes of citizens, such as parents, should have similar high standards for obvious reasons. But consider trial attorneys. These lawyers go into court with the sole objective of winning, along the way placing obstacles in the way of truth when they suspect that truth might jeopardize their clients' chances of winning. These actions do not display the ethics that justify lawyers being designated as true professionals or as officers of the court.

Now, more of a personal note. Throughout this writing, I have been concerned that opponents of what is advocated herein would believe that this book was written with a personal agenda in mind. If I have an agenda, it is not about trial attorneys per se. It is, however, about our present adversarial system of justice and its twin sister, the attorney-client privilege of communication. Trial lawyers who represent honest clients are shackled by these restraints. But a trial lawyer who represents a party in the wrong highly favors these hindrances to truth. To again avoid misunderstanding, the attorney-client privilege is entirely sound and fully justified when third part conflicts are not involved.

Because of our inexcusable adversarial court system and my distaste for it, in 1972 I began gathering material about our judicial system. I was annoyed with the poor reputation of the legal profession and with jokes about lawyers, some of which actually contained some element of truth. My father was a practicing attorney, so is my son, and, of course, so was I. Their reputation as well as mine is of great importance to me. Individually, lawyers are generally described as preeminent, especially in their obituaries, but as a group the legal profession suffers a shoddy reputation. Those lawyers that deny this surely must have their head in the sand, or maybe their greed is more important to them than their reputation.

My belief is that this unfavorable reputation is purely the result of the manner in which lawsuits and actions leading up to lawsuits are conducted. No valid reason exists for procedures that restrict truth and lawyers and judges who uphold them should be ashamed. Opponents will cite tradition and venerability as reasons for continuing the present system. These reasons, however, are hollow and unsubstantial. This book is a plea for leaders of the bar and the judiciary to rethink the US system of justice in order to truly create a legal profession, in action as well as in words. My sense is that the reputable public, many lawyers, many trial judges, some law professors, and even juries would applaud the reformation.

Lastly, whenever possible, I have tried to avoid discussing the financial consequences to the legal profession, if the adversarial system and the attorney-client privilege in conflict were eliminated. In part, this is because I don't know. I do know, however, that a truly responsible profession should not be making decisions or advocating or denying certain procedures based upon how it would affect their own pocketbook. A dream perhaps, but that is the way it should be.

BIBLIOGRAPHY

ABA Journal eReport: http://www.abanet.org/journal/ereport/

ABA membership report: ABAMEMBERSHIP@ABANET.ORG

Abel: Richard L. Abel. *American Lawyers*, New York, NY: Oxford University Press, 1989.

Advocate: *Iowa Advocate*, published twice a year by The University of Iowa College of Law, Iowa City, IA.

Brookhiser: Richard Brookhiser. *Rules of Civility*, New York, NY: The Free Press, 1997.

Bugliosi: Vincent Bugliosi. *Outrage The Five Reasons Why O. J. Simpson Got Away with Murder*, New York, NY: W. W. Norton & Company, 1996.

Crier: Catherine Crier. *The Case Against Lawyers*, New York, NY: Broadway Books, 2002.

Elias: Stephen Elias, Mary Randolph, Barbara Kate Repa, Ralph Warner. *Legal Breakdown*, Berkeley, CA, 1990.

Farnsworth: E. Allan Farnsworth. *An Introduction to the Legal System of the United States*, New York, NY: Oceana Publications, Inc., 1963.

Fleming: Macklin Fleming. *The Price of Perfect Justice*, New York, NY: Basic Books, Inc., 1974.

Friedman(1): Lawrence M. Friedman. *Total Justice*, New York, NY: Russell Sage Foundation, 1985.

Friedman(2): Lawrence M. Friedman. *A History of American Law*, Second Edition, New York, NY: A Touchstone Book, 1985.

Gazette: *The Gazette*, published daily by Gazette Communications, Inc., Cedar Rapids, IA.

Hickok: Eugene W. Hickok and Gary L. McDowell. *Justice vs. Law*, New York, NY: The Free Press, 1993.

Horn: Carl Horn III. *LawyerLife*, Chicago, IL: American Bar Association, 2003.

Imprimis: The national speech digest of Hillsdale College, 33 East College Street, Hillsdale, MI 49242.

Iowa Bar: hshipley@iowabar.org

Jacobson: William C. Jacobson, Ph.D. *We Are What We Were When*, Cedar Rapids, IA: WCJ33 Publishing L.L.C., 2004.

Jenkins: John A. Jenkins. *The Litigators*, New York, NY: Doubleday, 1989.

Journal: *ABA Journal*, published monthly by the American Bar Association, Chicago, IL.

Judicature: Published bimonthly by the American Judicature Society, Des Moines, IA.

Kagan: Robert A. Kagan. *Adversarial Legalism*, Cambridge, MA: Harvard University Press, 2001, 2003.

Kaminer: Wendy Kaminer. *It's All the Rage*, Reading, MA: Addison-Wesley Publishing Company, 1995.

Katz: Roberta R.Katz with Philip Gold. *Justice Matters*, Seattle, WA: Discovery Institute, 1997.

Knight: Alfred H. Knight. *The Life of the Law*, New York, NY: Crown Publishers, Inc., 1996.

Landsman: Stephan Landsman. *Readings on Adversarial Justice: The American Approach to Adjudication*, St. Paul, MN: West Publishing Co., 1988.

Lawyer: *The Iowa Lawyer*, published monthly by The Iowa State Bar Association, Des Moines, IA.

Neely: Richard Neely. *Why Courts Don't Work*, New York, NY: McGraw-Hill Book Company, 1982, 1983.

Newsweek: *Newsweek*, published weekly by Newsweek, Inc. New York, NY.

Olson: Walter K. Olson. *The Litigation Explosion*, New York, NY: Truman Talley Books/Plume, 1992.

Parade: *Parade*, published weekly by Parade Publications New York, NY.

Posner: Richard A. Posner. *The Problems of Jurisprudence*, Cambridge, MA: Harvard University Press, 1990.

Post: C. Gordon Post. *An Introduction to the Law*, Englewood Cliffs, N. J.: Prentice-Hall, Inc., 1963.

Pound: *The Causes of Popular Dissatisfaction with the Administration of Justice* by Roscoe Pound, Reports of the American Bar Association, Vol. XXIX, 1906, Part 1, p. 395.

Rawls: John Rawls. *A Theory of Justice*, Cambridge, MA: Harvard University Press, 1971.

Rembar: Charles Rembar. *The Law of the Land*, New York, NY: Simon and Schuster, 1980.

Rothwax: Harold J. Rothwax. *Guilty The Collapse of Criminal Justice*, New York, NY: Warner Books, 1996.

Rules: *Model Rules of Professional Conduct*, 2002 Edition, Chicago, IL: American Bar Association, 2002.

Spence: Gerry Spence. *With Justice for None*, New York, NY: Times Books, 1989.

Yerrid: C. Steven Yerrid. *When Justice Prevails*, New York, NY: Yorkville Press, 2003.

INDEX